The Big Bold Mindset

The Big Bold Mindset

Rethinking the rules of leadership

Caspar Craven

ISBN: 978-1-8381001-1-7

Cover design by Jemima Giffard-Taylor
Edited by Elaine O'Neill

DEDICATION

This book is dedicated to my family team who have shaped me, challenged me and encouraged me in more ways than they will ever realise.

Thank you.

Table of Contents

Introduction **1**

The Age of Disruption *2*

How to Approach this Book *4*

Why Me? *9*

Why Not the Big Bold Mindset? *10*

Your Invitation *11*

The Big Bold Steps **13**

Theme 1: Thinking Bigger **14**

Chapter 1 – Figure Out Focus **15**

Past Present Future *16*

Where Are You? *18*

The Science of Perspective *18*

Stuck in Unhealthy Conflict *20*

Big Bold Leaders *21*

Wear Different Hats *22*

Invite to Action *24*

Chapter 2 – Redraw the Charts **25**

Running Aground *26*

Where Are You? *26*

The Science of Disruption *27*

Avoiding a Shipwreck *29*

Big Bold Leaders *30*

Your Fresh Set of Charts *31*

Chapter 3: Challenge the Impossible **35**

Opinions vs Facts 36

Where Are You? 37

Change Resistant 38

Test Quickly and Cheaply 39

Big Bold Leaders 41

Aim High 43

Chapter 4 – Bolster Your Belief **45**

Specifically, Deliberately and Consciously 46

Where Are You? 46

The Science of Belief 47

Why Bother? 48

Big Bold Leaders 49

What's the Probability of Success? 50

Belief Construction in Progress 51

Theme 2: Leading Bigger **54**

Chapter 5 – Diversify Your Influence **55**

What You See Is All There Is 56

Where Are You? 56

The Science of Influence 59

Unhealthy Thoughts 60

Big Bold Leaders 61

A Social Experiment 63

Cull the Crosses 65

Line of Sight 65

Under Control 66

Chapter 6 – Construct Your Identity **69**

What Self Will You Be Today? *70*

Where Are You? *71*

The Science of Identity *71*

Big Bold Leaders *73*

How to Flex *74*

Visualise Reality *76*

Deliberately Construct *78*

Chapter 7 – Rewrite the Narrative **81**

Write a Fresh Story *82*

Where Are You? *83*

The Science of Support *84*

Painfully Distracted *85*

Big Bold Leaders *86*

Deep Listening *87*

Your Chart to the Future *92*

Chapter 8 – Direct Your Attention **95**

Setting Intention *97*

Where Are You? *98*

The Science of Attention *99*

Big Bold Leaders *101*

The Deep Work Checklist *102*

Get Focused *104*

Theme 3: Bigger Together **106**

Chapter 9 – Put People First **107**

Focused on the Wrong Thing 108

Where Are You? 110

The Science of Performance 111

It's All a Transaction 112

Big Bold Leaders 113

Putting People First 114

Chapter 10 – Agree on Values **119**

Where Are You? 121

The Science of Culture 123

Values Done Badly 124

Big Bold Leaders 125

Values to Create Growth 127

Begin at Home 128

Better Conversations at Work 130

Chapter 11 – Unleash Your Superpowers **133**

Centre of the World Thinking 134

Where Are You? 135

The Science of Self-Awareness 136

Stuck in a Rut 138

Big Bold Leaders 139

Be More Human 140

Vulnerable Conversations 141

The Superpowers Email 142

Celebrating Differences 143

Chapter 12 – Build Your Trust **145**

Where Are You? 147

The Science of Trust 148

Undermining Trust 150

Big Bold Leaders 150

Theme 4: Bigger by the Day **156**

Chapter 13 – Inch Yourself Forward **157**

Inch by Inch 158

Where Are You? 159

The Math of Marginal Gains 160

Failing to Reach the South Pole 161

Big Bold Leaders 162

Change Happens in the Calendar 163

It's Not a Sprint 166

Chapter 14 – Harness Your Habits **169**

What's Changed 170

Where Are You? 171

The Science of Habit 172

The Impact of Inaction 174

Optimised Leadership 175

The Habits Chart 176

Experiment with Everything 177

How Long Do You Want to Live? 179

Chapter 15 – Invest in Learning **181**

The Growth Mindset 184

Where Are You? 187

The Science of Adaptability 188

Big Bold Leaders 189
Stuck in a Loop 191
Sharpen your Learning Muscle 192
One Stroke at a Time 193

Chapter 16 – Push Past Perfect 197
Lightly Held to Tightly Held 199
Where Are You? 200
The Science of Perfectionism 200
Missing the Boat 203
Big Bold Leaders 204
Challenge Yourself 206
Thoughtful Disagreement 207
Better Decisions 208

Theme 5: Bigger Resilience 210

Chapter 17 – Strengthen with Safety 211
What Lies Beneath the Surface? 212
Where Are You? 213
The Science of Safety 214
Find the Truth 217
Big Bold Leaders 217
The Journey to Safer 219
Unlock the Benefits 221

Chapter 18 – Master Your Emotions 223
Candid Self Disclosure 226
Where Are You? 228
The Science of Emotions 229

Stuck in the Past 230
Big Bold Leaders 231
We're all a Work In Progress 232
The Never-Ending Journey 236
Chapter 19 – Calculate Your Risks **239**
What's the Real Risk? 240
Where Are You? 242
The Science of Bias 243
Big Bold (AI) Leaders 246
The Devil is in the Detail 248
Take Ownership 250
Chapter 20 – Create Through Conflict **253**
Grappling with the Issue 254
Where Are You? 255
The Science of Conflict 257
Wasted Potential 259
Big Bold Leaders 260
Reflection, Feedback and Action 262
Grapple Forward 264
The Final Step **267**
Chapter 21 – Adventure Beyond the Cognitive **269**
My Journey Beyond Cognitive 272
Caspar, You Do Know There's More Than Talk Therapy, Right? 273
The Trouble with Thinking 274
Where Are You? 275

The Rational Brain and The Emotional Brain 276
Trauma Touches Us All 279
How Experiences Shape Us 280
Unlocking Past Emotions 281
Experiment for Yourself 283

Conclusion **285**
What Influences Your World? 286
Big Bold Characteristics 286
Making an Impact 287
What Now? 290
Accelerating Action 290
My Wish for You 291

Resources **293**
Books 293
Articles and reports 295
Interviews 299
Websites 299

Acknowledgments

This book is written with deep appreciation to everyone who has shared my journey in business, in life and on my adventures. The stories shared and insights discovered have been shaped by the people I have had the privilege to learn from along the way.

I have met many inspiring people, too many to name individually, who have helped me learn what it takes to think bigger and bolder than I could ever have imagined.

My journey literally could not have been possible without my family and friends. Their patience while I painstakingly learnt these lessons has meant the world to me. My family, more than anyone else, has shown me the value of thinking bigger and bolder.

This book would not have happened without the expert support and guidance of Elaine O'Neill and my wife Nichola. Together, they have helped me to turn the stories, research ideas and insights into a readable structure.

Leadership happens at all levels and I have written this book with the primary intention of encouraging all leaders, and the teams they are part of, to develop a fresh mindset, a fresh way of thinking that is sustainable and actually sticks. Not just the latest passing fad.

Whether you are the most senior or junior member of a team, you will face challenges on your journey. My hope is that you will find insights and wisdom in these pages. Use this book to support and guide you to develop the mindset to take and achieve what many others dismiss as impossible.

To thinking bigger and bolder more than you ever thought possible.

Caspar Craven July 2023

Introduction

What does it take to be a successful leader today?

To lead in times of exponential change where challenges come from every direction.

To be the kind of leader who makes a real difference to the customers they serve and the people they work with.

I believe this needs a *different* type of leader.

It's not the leader who always knows best. It's not the leader using outdated approaches and ways of thinking. It's not the leader who lacks the humility and ability to own their mistakes. It's not the leader with a closed mind.

We need leaders who *think* differently.

Leaders who challenge the status quo.

Leaders who don't apply linear thinking to exponential problems.

I believe this is a leader who develops a Big Bold Mindset.

The age of focusing on incremental growth is over.

The age of thinking bigger and bolder is here.

It's here to stay.

If you do what those before you have done, you run the very real risk of being left behind.

Chances are, if you're an ambitious leader, you don't need convincing to think bigger and bolder.

You've already come to the conclusion that there is no other way.

The Age of Disruption

I cannot think of a single sector that is not being disrupted at this moment in time. Not one. There is disruption on every front: AI, Robotics, Big Data, Automation, The Metaverse, Exponential Technologies, Longevity Science, Genetics, the list goes on.

There are fascinating, exhilarating, and breath-taking advances in a huge number of fields, all happening at the same time.

You, like I, will be in doubt that we are at a tipping point in the world.

It throws into very sharp contrast the old model I cut my teeth on when I entered the working world in the early 1990s.

Back then, we had the fixed world model, where we could confidently say, "let's grow by 10% or 20% based on what we did last year".

That world is gone, long gone, and yet many people don't realise it.

I truly believe that if you *plan* to be in the business you are in today, in three years' time, you won't be in business.

Nimble upstart renegades eye every single revenue line of large corporates, figuring out ways to disrupt them.

This was written about at length by Clayton Christen in the *Innovator's Dilemma*.

Incumbents face challengers from outside the sector.

Spotify wasn't created by someone in the music sector.

AirBnB wasn't created by someone in the hotel sector.

Tesla wasn't created by someone in the auto sector.

We have no choice but to think bigger and bolder in order to disrupt our own industries, before someone else does.

We need a fresh set of strategies.

We need a Big Bold Mindset.

We have no choice but to think big and bold, to think 5x, 10x or perhaps 100x or more.

If we don't, someone else certainly will, and we risk being left behind.

I truly believe opportunities are never lost - they are simply discovered by someone else.

It's about imagining the future and being super clear on where you want to go, either as a team or individually.

It's about imagining a radically different world.

In his work on Digital Disruption, Professor Kamal Munir at the University of Cambridge recommends a process that has many similarities.

To paraphrase his recommendations, to adapt to a world that is being continually disrupted world, we must:

'Imagine the world in 5 years.
Imagine it without what you do today.
What does it look like?
Where are the trends pointing to?
Who are the players?
Now imagine where you'd like to be and orient your model to that.'

This is serious work.

It's taking your best bet on the future and spending time thinking about it and orienting your strategy around it.

The more clearly you can see it, the more tangible your plans can be to make it happen.

The *challenge* of course is that our minds are riddled with notions from the past - old ideas, embedded beliefs, inherited patterns of thinking.

How to Approach this Book

To get the most out of the *Big Bold Mindset*, you'll need to harness some key characteristics.

The raw ingredients for thinking bigger and bolder.

The higher we rise in our professional lives, the more likely it is that we run the risk of developing ingrained ways of thinking, rather than challenging our thought processes.

While your experience is worth its weight in gold, it's about igniting a set of innate human characteristics. It's about being as open minded as you can.

You already have a collection of these characteristics embodying the Big Bold Mindset approach to life. It's your invitation to assimilate your courageous inquiring self along with your sage leadership qualities.

As you read this book, be curious, be creative, ask questions, devour everything you learn; Become hungry for knowledge.

To really explore curiosity, you have to be humble. In this ever-changing world, you cannot know everything, no matter how long you've been in business. Allow yourself to be a novice.

Every chapter is going to invite you to experiment with what you've learned. The more curious you are, the more adventurous your experiments will become. Let yourself have fun.

I encourage you to step outside your comfort zone. To get more comfortable feeling uncomfortable. This is where real growth happens.

Here's the challenge with that and also the way round it. It's much easier to step into discomfort when we feel safe in our environment, when we feel supported and have a nurturing environment.

Trickier when we don't feel safe and there is a high degree of uncertainty and anxiety in our world.

Harvard's Amy Edmondson coined the term 'psychological safety' in a 1999 journal article exploring its relationship with team learning and performance.

Psychological safety means an absence of interpersonal fear.

Some people feel safer at home.

Some people feel safer at work.

And of course, sadly, some people do not feel safe in either situation.

The ideas, tools and skills I am inviting you to develop can be used either at work or home.

I suggest you develop them in the environment you feel safest in.

It's the place where you are most likely to develop them by stepping outside of that comfort zone.

I developed many of my Big Bold Mindset skills at home.

Once I developed and honed my skills at home, I felt more comfortable to take them to work and really use them there. It was my journey to becoming the best leader I had ever been.

Choose where you feel safest and sharpen your skills there.

When considering any new idea, I always seek to approach it with humility.

People with a Big Bold Mindset tend to be comfortable admitting they don't know the answers. They are open minded and seek out the wisdom they need and are honest about the gaps they have.

Everything changed for me, when I went from saying *"I'm right" to "How do I know I'm right?"*

These are the words of Ray Dalio, founder of the world's largest hedge fund, Bridgewater Associates to describe the crucial mindset shift he needed on his journey from struggling to succeeding.

None of us have enough lifetimes to know all the information and insights we will ever need. It's that humility we need to appreciate our own limitations, to be open minded to the notion that our current way of thinking might not be the best way.

The Big Bold Mindset is always willing to challenge the status quo and dare to be different.

If you do what you've always done, you will get what you've always got.

People with a Big Bold Mindset are not afraid of being wrong, not afraid of looking at things in a different way and probing for answers to: why is it this way? Is there a better way? Is there another way?

Leaders with a Big Bold Mindset know the future looks different and that there are no certainties. They know they will fail. They know they will fail a lot.

They choose to approach the journey with a sense of experimentation. They know they will have to experiment a lot and iterate their way towards the future.

Each successive experiment contains clues as to the next one. It's a journey that never ends.

The Big Bold Mindset invites reflection. Leaders who take the time to reflect and notice what worked well and what didn't work so well. These reflections are then used to shape the hypothesis for the next experiment.

Unless we study and reflect on the past, we are destined to keep making the same mistakes and repeating the same patterns into the future.

Every leader I've met with a Big Bold Mindset realises they can't do it on their own. They need a team of people. People who can compensate for where they are weak.

Further, those leaders have all arrived at the insight that people only do things for their own reasons and not the reasons of the leader.

It's based on this understanding, that leaders with a big bold mindset know that it is crucial to listen to, engage with, and to nurture people in their team.

When you put people first, the results will follow. This is something I see big bold leaders the world over understanding at their core.

Tomorrow only happens because of what we do today.

Dreamers love imagining the future and becoming excited about the possibilities.

And equally, dreaming without relentless action will remain just a dream.

Every single person who has achieved anything big and bold has an ability to shuttle between the big picture out there in the future and then the immediate actions, goals and small steps to make it happen.

Spend a day in the company of any accomplished senior leader on a mission and it will be hard to miss the strong bias towards action.

It's simply a case of how quickly you can run the experiments needed, and to take the insights from them to make progress towards your goal.

One mentor ingrained in me the question:

“What have I done today to move meaningfully and measurably closer to my goal today?”

Why Me?

Who am I to write this book?

I’ve disrupted my life on more than one occasion both at work and at home.

In the working world, I’ve worn the hats of:

- Commercial Fisherman
- Chartered Accountant
- KPMG Associate Director
- CFO
- Serial Entrepreneur, and
- Motivational Leadership Speaker.

Outside work I’ve sailed around the world, twice.
The first time on the world’s toughest yacht race and the second time with my wife and three children under the age of 10.

Over the past decade, I’ve developed an obsession with what it takes to set, tackle, and achieve big bold goals.

I've researched, interviewed, and met some of the most impressive leaders on our planet.

Success leaves clues. What I share in these pages is the fusion of the clues, the patterns that I've observed and studied together with my own experiences.

My trademark is delivering thought-provoking talks and ideas on how to achieve your Big Bold Goals. I speak at between 50 and 100 events per year for global leaders including Burberry, Johnson and Johnson, Amazon and many more.

I wasn't always this way.

Until my early thirties, I played it safe at work.

It was when both my work and home life started failing that I started to rethink my approach and step beyond my comfort zone.

Although I didn't realise it at the time, I applied the Big Bold Mindset to both my areas of my life and created dramatically different results.

This is a story I share in my previous books, *Be More Human* and *Where the Magic Happens*.

Why Not the Big Bold Mindset?

Leaving aside the clear conclusion that it's better to be the disruptor than the disrupted, there are several other good reasons to get on the front foot with the Big Bold Mindset.

You're more likely to attract the best talent, especially if there's a clear and important purpose to your work.

And perhaps most importantly, it's more fun. We spend so much of our time at work, that finding a way to enjoy it is beneficial for you, for everyone you work with, and for your family too.

If you've reached this far, we are likely to be kindred spirits wanting to make a difference by not just showing up to make up the numbers.

I also know that I don't really need to convince you to develop a big bold mindset, I just need to share the best of what I've discovered and the tools and techniques that I've found helpful.

Your Invitation

This book is your invitation to think differently.

To think bigger and bolder than you've ever done before.

It's intended to be thought-provoking. It's intended to be challenging.

It's a book about mindset, your mindset.

A mindset is defined as a way of thinking, especially a habitual way of thinking.

There are very good reasons why you might want to change your habitual thinking and think differently. This is an important area we will explore together.

We will go deeper, much deeper into exploring frameworks, tools and ideas which will help you on your journey.

This book is written primarily for people with ambition.

For senior leaders, for people aspiring to be senior leaders.

People who want to seize opportunities, take initiatives and move things forward.

It's written to provoke you.

Written to open you to different ideas and ways of thinking.

If you're an ambitious leader, chances are you've already read a good amount.

Much of the literature I've read is the *same old, same old* rehashed stories and ideas.

This is not intended to be one of those. It's intended to be a breath of fresh air.

It's been written how I think.

It's been written how I like to read.

Short and pithy.

I don't have much patience for waffle and verbose text.

I don't imagine you do as a leader, either?

I want to reach my point quickly so you can rapidly digest and quickly get into experimenting with the ideas.

The Big Bold Steps

Theme 1: Thinking Bigger

Every great leader is a dreamer first.

It's when we dream and imagine that we can begin to see what we can't see when we stuck in the day to day.

It's said that everything is created twice.

The first time in your mind.

The second time in reality.

Thinking bigger is the first step in embodying the Big Bold Mindset.

You've got to drop the shackles of the day to day, the shackles that can keep us thinking 'small'.

The next four chapters will show you how.

Use them to expand your horizon and become the disruptor your company needs.

Let them help you think bigger.

Chapter 1 – Figure Out Focus

"But we've always done it this way."

I could feel my frustration rising as I heard these resistant words once again.

I'd suggest a new idea, a fresh way of looking at things, some creative thoughts.

And very quickly it would be rebuffed with the mantra of "we've always done it this way".

I noticed the pattern at home first, when I'd suggest new plans for our family.

And once I noticed the pattern there, I saw the same thing playing out at work.

The pattern seemed to consistently play out the same way.

It bugged me.

I focused hard on the pattern and reflected.

Was it my tone of voice?

Was it my timing?

Was I raising the suggestion at the wrong time?

Was I overdoing the number of new ideas?

While all those things may well have been true, I happened on a thought that started to unlock a different pattern of thinking.

I started to wonder if we all looked at time in the same way. Have you ever caught yourself saying things like?

"That person is so stuck in the past."

Or

"'That person seems to be always looking for the next big idea - they have a new idea every day and seem to forget what they said last week."

Past Present Future

I reflected on the unconscious biases we all have and the impact it has on our communication with others. You know, those biases that sit just beneath the surface, that if revealed, could make our conversations just a little bit easier.

This thought developed into a deceptively simple question:

If you examine where you put your time, energy and focus, what percentage is directed at the past, what percentage at the present and what percentage at the future?

I was experiment subject number one as I questioned myself.

My answer was 0-10-90.

I realised I spent 0% of the time focused on the past, 10% in the present and 90% in the future. That was my nature: always thinking about what was coming next; the next audacious goal, plans I could make happen, exciting things that were changing.

Was it just me thinking like this?

My wife was experiment subject number two.

Her answers stopped me in my tracks.

She replied 50-30-20.

As in 50% focused on the past, 30% in the present, and 20% in the future.

A moment of insight

That one question revealed the obvious truth that we all look at the world very differently. We all have our own 'time' biases that are shaped by our experiences of the world.

It's human to fall into the trap of thinking the world sees things the same way that you do.

They don't.

We all see the world through our own lens.

It's when we compare and reflect the lenses, we start to understand both ourselves and others better.

It's this sharing, this vulnerability, this level of understanding that can be a powerful key to unlocking how we work together better and how we can better navigate conflicts and different ways to tackle the hard problems in front of us.

The light bulb came on as I realised that my wife and I were actually talking about completely different things, despite thinking we were on the same page.

I was leaning virtually 5 times more into the future (90%), while she only spent 20% of her energy there. Half of her focus was on the past, while none of mine was directed there.

It suddenly became blindingly obvious why we were having so many arguments at that time!

Where Are You?

Just pause reading right now and reflect on your own focus.

If you examine where you put your time, energy, and focus, what percentage is directed at the past, how much in the present and how much towards the future?

Don't overthink it. Just scribble down your numbers.

There are no right or wrong answers here.

This is quite simply a tool for understanding yourself better.

We'll explore how you can use this tool shortly, but for now just make a note of your numbers.

The Science of Perspective

There are many reasons why we might look at time differently. One very powerful insight comes from the work of psychiatrist Bessel van der Kolk, which he shares in his bestselling book, *The Body Keeps the Score.*

The core notion he explores is that every single person has experienced events across their life, events that leave an emotional imprint.

These experiences shape our minds and how we look at the world. Van der Kolk explains why each of us are shaped differently by the events that have occurred, noting the distinction between the cognitive part of the brain and emotional centres in the brain.

In particular, van der Kolk's work focuses on trauma and the lasting emotional response that often results from living through a distressing event.

Let's consider this point when we think about where someone's time bias lies.

We can do this by returning to the phrase "someone is living in the past?"

It's a very real thing, someone who hasn't fully processed an emotional event remains trapped in the past. The slightest trigger can bring back that memory, as though it is happening to them right now.

Take me as an example. I experienced some traumatic events early in my life and my approach was always that it will be better in the future. If you will, my psychological pattern was to escape the present into the future where everything was better than the moment I was living in.

Each of us has a very different psychological profile that causes us to look at the world differently. I'm not seeking to explain all the reasons why we view things differently. It's simply enough to understand that based on our unique experiences, we just do.

For now, consider your Past/Present/Future percentages, and what could have caused you to focus more in one area than another.

Then step back and realise how unconscious that behaviour is for you. Only then can you understand how truly unconscious it is for another. So, instead of glorifying one mindset over another, you can see them for what they are: potential protective mechanisms for daily life.

Stuck in Unhealthy Conflict

When it comes to our mind that we need to achieve a Big Bold Mindset, the more energy and focus we can use to tackle the hard problems, the more likely we are to make progress.

All too often though we make a bonfire of our productive energy by getting caught up in conflicts. Conflicts that could potentially be simply resolved by better understanding the reality that different people look at things differently.

Conflict takes different forms.

There is healthy conflict, where people grapple and struggle together to solve hard problems.

And unhealthy conflict where you never seem to reach the bottom of where the differences are.

Healthy conflict can energise us. Unhealthy conflict can drain us. It's important we choose wisely.

Understanding time bias is one tool to have in your tool kit to avoid being stuck in repeating patterns of unhealthy conflict.

Understanding someone else's perspective can reframe conflict to energise a situation.

It's a foundational part of the Big Bold Mindset.

Big Bold Leaders

In the keynote talks I give to business audiences around the world, I always ask people to share their Past / Present / Future numbers.

Every time the feedback is the same. The results show a huge variation across the room. Put simply, we don't all view time in the same way and we all have an underlying bias.

How do successful leaders with a Big Bold Mindset view time?

My experience shows me that they develop what I call *conscious time dexterity*. Rather than being stuck on a particular default, they become aware of their bias and then consciously flex around it.

It's an ability to look to the future to check you're headed in the right direction, to be able to reflect and learn from the past, and then return to the present and action required to move forward.

John Stapleton, founder of the 'fresh soup' supermarket movement through The Covent Garden Soup company, told me he spends 20% focusing on the past, 60% on the present, and 20% on the future:

" You need to spend time imagining the future, you need to spend time reflecting on past experiments and learning from them and then to get focused on the present. Today is the time that you have and it's time to make things happen."

Stapleton is not alone among the many of the successful leaders I've spoken to. I see a healthy amount of future focus, a healthy amount of past focus for reflection, with the largest percentage in the present, focused on what needs to happen now to move the dial.

My challenge to you is to increase your conscious time dexterity. That is your ability to consciously shuttle between the different time lenses.

It's about becoming more aware of how you think about time so that you can more easily switch out of your default mode.

Wear Different Hats

In my talks and the workshops our team delivers, I have a set of three coloured hats.

The Blue Hat has the word Past on it.

The Green Hat has the word Present.

The Black Hat has the word Future.

Using the hats as prompts, I invite the audience to think through one particular lens.

I like to start in the Future wearing the Black Hat. Let's all go out into the future. For now, we're just going to park the past, leave the present where it is today and transport ourselves to the future. Some people will find this easy (the future focused people of the group), and others may find it more challenging (the past and present focused people).

All we are seeking to do is to align our thinking and, in this exercise, get the room of people looking *in the same direction, at the same time.*

Using the future hat is a very useful exercise to help us write the shared story of the future, to map out what the future big bold goals look like without focusing on the present and the past. I like to think of this as a reality disconnect where all we want to do is unleash our imaginations.

Why do I do this? I find that if we try to address all the 'how do we do this questions' at the same time as imagining a bigger future, we get overwhelmed because there is no way to answer all the hard questions at the same time as working out what the future looks like.

The very real risk then is that teams scale back the size of their ambition until they reach a point where they have the answers to grow by a much smaller amount. This is exactly what we don't want!

Once we have imagined a bigger, bolder future, we then take a break and switch gears.

I will then put on the Past hat, the Blue hat. I want the team to spend time reflecting on the past.

What experiments have we run and what have we learnt from them?

What have we learnt about what our customers want?

What have we learnt about how we best operate as a team?

What can you and your team learn from your past experiments?

And finally, I put on the Green Hat. We're now in the present. We know where we want to go in the future. We know what we have learnt from the past. What are the resources we have today and how can we make best use of these resources to start to map our way towards the future.

What projects and ideas can we experiment with?

Tomorrow only happens because of what we do today.

This is about setting out the plans and experiments and setting aside regular time to review what insights those experiments are creating.

Through the use of the coloured hats, it creates a more structured conversation and avoids falling into the obvious trap of "let's do this" vs "we've always done it this way", and I find it helps defuse conflicts.

Invite to Action

I invite you to have a conversation with your team at home or at work. Share your Past Present Future numbers with others and listen deeply to what others are saying and why their focus is where it is.

This act of sharing, listening and being open about something personal to each of us is also powerful for trust building, as we get to know ourselves and others better.

This is about having better conversations so that together as a team we can better navigate to a more exciting place in the future.

Chapter 2 – Redraw the Charts

"We're losing to the competition, our margins are being shredded, and we're struggling to retain good people."

Have you ever been in this situation?

Perhaps you or someone you know is in this situation right now?

I've certainly been in this situation, and moreover, these are reflective of many frank conversations I am, often party to from large established companies who are being challenged on many fronts.

Companies both big and small are busy being disrupted.

Disrupted by new market entrants innovating quickly, by new technologies, by newcomers who refuse to bow to the received wisdom about "how things are done" in your sector.

Every business has a choice.

It can wait to be disrupted by others or it can develop a Big Bold Mindset and become a disruptor.

Being on the back foot in a business getting hammered by an upstart is frankly, a miserable place to be.

So, what's the answer?

Running Aground

Lying off the north coast of the Isthmus of Panama, just east of the Panama Canal are the San Blas Islands, an archipelago comprising around 365 islands.

Some years ago, I sailed there and was struck by the number of boats which had run aground on the coral reefs surrounding the islands.

On investigation, the reason quickly became apparent.

The nautical charts for the area were last updated several hundred years ago by Captain Cook.

In short, they were out of date and inaccurate and no doubt played a vital part in sending many of these boats to their final resting place.

The mental models and approaches our leaders are using today are similar to Captain Cook's charts.

Many leaders out there are trying to solve the problems of today with the solutions of yesterday. Simply put, they are trying to navigate a new world using an old set of charts.

If you last studied leadership, mindset and change even just five years ago, you are way out of date. Even more so if your skills were last updated, 10, 20, 30 or 40 years ago.

Where Are You?

Just pause reading right now and reflect on when you last thought about the charts that you are mentally using? When were they last upgraded? Are they fresh or dated? What books are you referencing? How long ago were they written?

The Science of Disruption

Fifty years ago, if a company made its way onto the Fortune 500 list, it would expect to stay there for 75 years. That's now down to 15 years and continues to decline.

Professor Kamal Munir at Cambridge Judge Business School teaches organisations on how to lead in an age of disruption.

To succeed, he argues, businesses need to orientate around the future.

The challenge is that too much thinking inside organisations is orientated around the past or the present.

The equivalent of Captain Cook's old set of charts.

To be able to create an effective strategy for the future, it is essential that you begin by taking yourself out of the equation and think how a re-imagined world may look like in five years' time.

In this world, one imagines what the ecosystem will look like.

What are the trends, what has changed, who are the players, what does this world look like?

One creates this imagined world by examining the trends you can observe today and formulating your best bet of what the future will look like.

Once you have drawn your picture of the future, then form an opinion about where the value will accrue.

What parts of that picture are likely to be commoditised?

What will you want to avoid?

Which parts of the picture will end up being the most valuable parts?

With your value epicentre in place, then and only then can you look at how you position yourself in the ecosystem.

This is where you then reflect on the assets you have, the cards your organisation is holding and begin to map your story from the future.

This type of thinking requires a shift in collective mindset, which can be challenging.

Many people find it hard to detach from the reality of today and too many people are building their strategies of the future without appropriately considering how the future will look.

They are stuck with thinking about the assets and strengths of their organisation today, not the environment the business will be sitting in.

Part of this shows up as overconfidence on past successes.

The thinking that goes along the lines of 'we're great because of [insert whatever strengths you have today].'

It is this past focus and an inability to flex mindsets that can play a pivotal role in the downfall of many leading organisations.

Avoiding a Shipwreck

Disruption is happening in plain sight around the world as Artificial Intelligence (AI) is applied across industries.

The online search market, dominated by Google for the past two decades, is set to change rapidly as it becomes augmented by AI.

Nothing ever stands still, and this rate of disruption is increasing exponentially.

Clayton Christensen's work on disruptive innovation explored the ways disruptors enter and overtake industries.

At the core of the disruption dilemma, is that it takes real courage to adopt a Big Bold Mindset. It means finding products and services that disrupt your current business methods.

A senior banking executive shared with me the story of how one large established bank created their own version of a low-cost application for currency exchange.

The head of currency pulled the plug on the project as it would have disrupted his very profitable traditional currency exchange business.

That project halt cost the bank greatly, as non-banking disruptors were already in the wings launching their own low-cost exchange apps.

The safe move was the wrong move.

History shows that falling into the "too busy to think about it", "too busy to plan for it", "too busy to act on it" is a dangerous place to be.

Big Bold Leaders

Leaders who exemplify the Big Bold Mindset start with engaging hearts and minds.

They are the ones who inspire their teams with an exciting story of the future.

Kevin Gaskell was 32 when he was appointed managing director of Porsche when it was on the brink of bankruptcy and, in less than five years turned it round to become the UK's most profitable car company.

He later moved to BMW where he was responsible for 500% increase in profitability and a record growth of 80% in sales.

Gaskell has openly shared the process that worked for him on numerous occasions to turn around struggling businesses and launch new early-stage ventures.

The starting point is to ditch traditional thinking of 5 or 10% growth, and to focus on what can create 5x, 10x or even 100x growth.

Gaskell's process involves starting in the future to imagine what we will see, hear, and feel and to create what he calls "the one version of the truth", the picture in the minds of the team that everyone agrees on.

The work then focuses on what are all the different projects needed in order to deliver world class results.

Since there will always be more projects to deliver than time and resources allow, the process prioritises those that are the most important and impactful.

These are converted into 50-day sprints where the team can rapidly run the experiments to solve the most pressing issues and introduce fresh thinking to solve hard problems.

Leaders with a Big Bold Mindset don't hang around.

They are the ones who are moving fast, taking action, and running lots of experiments.

It was Darwin who revealed those who survive aren't the strongest, but those who adapt are the fastest.

Jeff Bezos put it succinctly:" *Our success at Amazon is a function of how many experiments we do per year, per month, per week. Being wrong might hurt you a bit. Being slow will kill you."*

In the world of the Big Bold Mindset, there is scant respect for traditional 'industry boundaries' or 'core competencies'. This inquiring ambitious mindset is always looking at ways to do things differently.

Your Fresh Set of Charts

Who's thinking big and bold in your team?

Is it someone?

Is it no-one?

Who's investing in cultivating a Big Bold Mindset, who has a senior enough voice to make a difference?

And how do you develop the culture transformation to achieve that shift across an entire organisation?

Operating with a Big Bold Mindset means taking the lead and positively disrupting yourself.

Rather than hanging on to what you have today, you take the lead and find ways to disrupt your own market.

Is it risky?

Yes, it is. But it's a far bigger risk to try and hold onto an old marketplace and wait it out until you are disrupted by someone else.

The good news is, that developing a Big Bold Mindset is a learnable skill set and there will be a number of people inside your organisation keen to embrace a new mindset.

This is your challenge

Inspire yourself with a bigger bolder story of the future.

Enthusiasm is infectious and it's hard to inspire others if you don't feel inspired yourself.

Put on the Future hat and transport yourself five years from now.

What will you see, hear, and feel?

Detach yourself from the reality of today.

Forget about being a manager and focus on being a leader.

Be the leader, the author of your own story and imagine what a more exciting world looks like.

Don't worry for now about how you might achieve it, or practical challenges and issues; we'll cover that in the next chapter.

Simply imagine and dream what that different world looks like.

While you are there in the future, use words and pictures to capture and detail what you see.

Make it as vivid and real as you can.

This is about developing your mindset, your skill to think bigger and bolder than you've ever done before.

Get comfortable developing and flex your skills in this space,

Imagine.

Leadership at its simplest involves three steps.

The first step is to imagine a future that is better than today.

The second is to see the reality of today, not how you wish it was but how it really is.

The third is to develop an action plan that closes the gap between today and tomorrow.

They are very distinct steps and need to be done separately rather than at the same time.

Leading yourself comes before leading others.

This exercise of creating an exciting story in the future is a skill. Like all skills, it needs practice to develop proficiency.

Many people, me included, developed these skills in my home life by imagining a better future.

Others develop these skills at work.

It doesn't really matter where you develop the skill of creating an inspiring story of the future, just let it become a vital element in shaping your Big Bold Mindset.

Chapter 3: Challenge the Impossible

Have you ever had a brilliant idea, something you got really excited about?

And then very quickly you started thinking about all the reasons why it couldn't work.

You got overwhelmed, thought it was impossible and before you knew it, you'd talked yourself out of the idea and carried on with life and work as it was before.

Worse still, a year down the line, you discovered someone else turned that same idea into a successful one?

Perhaps, you even got as far as vocalising that idea, where it was met with the response, "that's crazy, it's impossible, there's no way that can happen".

It's all too easy to let the voices, yours and others, drown out what could be the start of something brilliant.

It's all too easy to carry on as you were before, never challenging the status quo.

Leaders exhibiting a Big Bold Mindset find ways to navigate through this pitfall.

They use a learnable approach that you and your team can develop to tackle bigger challenges.

Opinions vs Facts

Here's the challenge: sometimes, opinions are expressed so forcefully that they sound like facts.

But they're not, they are simply opinions, one person's view based on their experiences, which may or may not be relevant to the mission that you have in mind.

We listen to the opinions of others both because of our fear of criticism, and the size of the challenge that lays ahead of us.

We weigh up the risk of failure and decide how to make our next step.

How would you have responded to any of these situations:

- You're running AirBnB and a pandemic shuts down global travel - the driver underpinning the bedrock of your revenue.
- You're running Burberry and your brand has been tarnished by controversial associations, causing low-cost rip-offs to affect your bottom line.
- You're a car manufacturer who has been disrupted by Tesla and its rapid advances in developing electric-vehicle technology.

As you read this, there are no doubt many market challenges happening all around you that seem insurmountable.

That it's too hard to overcome, compete or tackle, so instead your team chooses an easier mountain to climb.

Many people have an understandable fear of being criticised, of having their ideas challenged and when presented with strong voices veer away from a big bold idea and back to *smaller safer steps*.

Our psychological programming absolutely has a part to play in how our belief systems have developed, and this is an area that I invite every reader to explore.

It is not that the challenge is too big, but that the potential for criticism feels too threatening. We mistake another's opinion as fact. We allow their summation of their own limitations to affect our own.

Where Are You?

Just pause reading right now and reflect on what plans you've discarded in the past because of loud voices? What have you lost because you've talked yourself out of action?

A simple question can reveal much.

How would you rate your comfortableness with criticism? On a scale of 1 to 100 where would you put it where 1 is "I loathe it" and 100 is "Bring it on"?

It's a complex area and taking the time to reflect on this and considering ways to become more comfortable with criticism will be time well spent.

I'm fairly certain that you'll have heard the words, "there's no such thing as failure, only feedback". If only these words carried all the way through and we truly ingrained them, then the world would be a very different place!

Change Resistant

Why is it as individuals and organisations we are resistant to change and challenging the way we have done things historically?

Writing in her 2020 book, Think Outside the Building, Professor Rosabeth Moss Kantar looks at why we can be so resistant to change.[1]

She considers some of the most common reasons why[2], reasons that are ingrained in human behaviour.

Excess uncertainty

If change feels like walking off a cliff blindfolded, then people will reject it. People will often prefer to remain mired in misery than to head toward an unknown. As the saying goes, "Better the devil you know than the devil you don't know.

Everything seems different

Change is meant to bring something different, but how different? We are creatures of habit. Routines become automatic, but change jolts us into consciousness, sometimes in uncomfortable ways. Too many differences can be distracting or confusing.

Surprise, surprise!

Decisions imposed on people suddenly, with no time to get used to the idea or prepare for the consequences, are generally resisted. It's always easier to say *No* than to say *Yes.*

---

[1]*Think Outside the Building: How Advanced Leaders Can Change the World One Smart Innovation at a Time*(Public Affairs, 2020)

[2] https://hbr.org/2012/09/ten-reasons-people-resist-chang

Concerns about competence

Can I do it? Change is resisted when it makes people feel stupid. They might express skepticism about whether the new idea could work, but down deep they are worried that their skills will be obsolete.

More work

Here is a universal challenge. Change is indeed more work. Those closest to the change in terms of designing and testing it are often overloaded,

Loss of control

Change interferes with autonomy and can make people feel that they've lost control over their territory.

Perhaps you recognise some of these feelings when you have been presented with change? To be a leader is to understand humans and to be able to help others on their journey.

The better you can understand the likely reactions, both for you and others, the better you can guide the path.

Test Quickly and Cheaply

Marc Randolph, Co-Founder of Netflix, is no stranger to impossible ideas.

In his book and podcast by the same name, *That Will Never Work,* he outlines his strategies for dealing with hard problems.

At the core of his thesis is that it's very difficult to tell a good idea from a bad idea and that the key is how quickly you can collide your ideas with reality.

He advocates figuring out ways to test the ideas as quickly and cheaply as possible, and that once you start this process, you find the ideas that will work and iterate your way forward with experiments.

One story is that of a college student who had the idea for a venture around peer-to-peer clothing rental.

He quickly dissuaded her from raising funds and hiring a CTO to develop a prototype project and went straight to the heart of the proposition.

His advice was to simply pin a sheet of paper to her door in the halls of residence with the words:

Want to borrow my clothes?

Knock.

Very quickly she would find out if there was demand for the idea. If there was interest, and provoked conversations, she would quickly find out what customer tastes were, pricing insights, how to deal with returns, dry cleaning and many other aspects that would be fundamental to the proposition.

It was the same approach that Randolph used to test the original idea for Netflix, loaning out DVDs by mail, which at the time had never been done before.

Within hours of coming up with the idea, they drove to a local store, bought a second-hand music CD, and mailed it in the post.

When it turned up the following day, it was experiment number 1 to show the fundamental premise of sending DVDs by mail could work.

In our quest for perfection, all too often we can be overthinking and searching for that one brilliant idea that never comes.

It's far better to start running experiments, knowing that most will fail, and that the insights will guide the way to something successful.

Big Bold Leaders

The single most useful tool I've developed for navigating my way through impossible challenges is a single sheet of paper.

A sheet of paper with a line down the middle.

On the left-hand side of the line write the word WHY. Reflect on why this challenge is important to you.

Really take the time to think about it and go as deep as you can into what's driving your desire for this challenge.

By definition, impossible challenges will be hard and there will be many obstacles on the path ahead.

If it's a weak reason WHY, it's easy to imagine the project running out of steam as you progress.

If it's a powerful engaging WHY, then reminding yourself of this when the going gets tough is a powerful tool to go deeper into problem-solving mode.

On the right-hand side of the page, write the word WHY NOT.

Here is the space to write down every single reason why this will fail. Don't hold back here.

You want to get a full list of all the reasons why this idea won't work.

All too often, what happens is we try to do this in our heads and quickly feel overwhelmed by the size of the challenge and give up.

Because we can't answer all those questions right now, it seems too hard.

The cognitive flip here is these WHY NOT reasons are quite simply our to-do list.

These are the challenges that we have to get clear on and figure out the answers to in order to be able to move forwards.

If we don't get clear on what challenges we need to overcome we have no hope of achieving our goals.

Once we have this list, rather than feeling emotionally overwhelmed and removing ourselves from the idea, we can focus on logically taking it one step at a time.

Gary Keller, author of The One Thing, has a very useful approach called: 'The Focusing Question' which is "What is the one thing I can do that makes everything else either easier or unnecessary?".

The question forces you to prioritise the most important problem to focus on solving.

It's impossible to have 27 number 1 priorities, so this approach helps to zone in on what the most important challenge is to solve right now.

Randolph from Netflix advocates spending 95% of your time on 5% of your problems.

Getting clear on which is the most important 5% is a skill requiring development.

It's very easy to be a busy fool working on lots of projects that are not going to move the dial.

Aim High

Michelangelo famously said the greater danger for most of us lies not in setting our aim too high and falling short; but in setting our aim too low and achieving our mark.

Where is your aim?

Could it be higher if you developed the skill set to face down bigger and bolder challenges?

What could happen if your mindset allowed you to embrace criticism, failure, and challenges at a higher level than it is today?

I'm not advocating throwing caution to the wind with wild-card ideas.

I want to invite you to sit comfortably with uncertainty and challenge.

I encourage the use of your valuable time and energy to devise experiments that can quickly home in on the biggest questions that need answering.

Chapter 4 – Bolster Your Belief

Have you ever had self-doubt about whether you can achieve a significant project, either on your own or as part of a team?

Have you ever felt uncertain and not sure that you can pull off the toughest challenge of your life, whatever that may be?

"Sometimes the mental gymnastics in your head cause you to not take your shot[3]." The words of Thasunda Brown Duckett, former CEO of Chase Consumer Banking.

Have you ever pulled back from taking your shot?

What does it take to create belief that we can actually make the shot?

And crucially what happens if we don't feel that way?

Is there a way to create belief?

It's a question I've grappled with many times and have often found myself feeling frustrated at the start of a big bold goal.

I've stared down the face of impossible, but did I actually believe it was possible?

---

[3] https://business.wisc.edu/news/leadership-gems-from-tiaa-ceo-thasunda-brown-duckett/

I can't say that I always did.

I've often wondered if there are concrete steps you can take to increase your belief in an idea, project, person, or team?

I now know better.

Specifically, Deliberately and Consciously

In all the conversations I've had with leaders exhibiting the Big Bold Mindset, this notion of belief regularly arises as being a crucial factor in being able to move forwards.

The notion I've come to hold true after much reflection, studying and many conversations, is that belief is something that can be created specifically, deliberately, and consciously.

The simplest analogy is that creating belief is a skill set, something that you can train yourself to do.

Like building a muscle, the more you train it and develop it, the stronger it gets.

Of course, having absolute belief is no guarantee that you will succeed, but it does stack the cards in your favour by meaning you are more likely to press on when the going gets tough.

Where Are You?

Cast your mind back to a time when you achieved something significant.

A big bold goal that was hard to achieve.

When you started on the journey achieving that goal, did you have absolute belief that you would achieve it?

Was there anything that you did either at the start of that journey or along the way that either increased or decreased your belief in yourself?

What repeatable elements could you note down that you can use to increase the belief you will successfully achieve your next big bold goal?

Different things work for different people and paying attention to what works well for you could be the single most important thing to grow your belief.

Put simply, if it worked before for you, make sure to do it again. If it doesn't work, avoid it.

The Science of Belief

Research published in 2020 in the Journal of Personality and Social Psychology [4] found that people's beliefs about their personality were effectively a self-fulfilling philosophy.

If the belief was that personality was fixed, there was low motivation to change, which of course led to no change.

Conversely, the belief that you can change, positively influenced the motivation to change, which ultimately caused the trait change.

---

[4]4 Yeager, D. S., Dweck, C. S., & Trzesniewski, K. H. (2020). An implicit theory of personality predicts motivation and goal progress across adulthood. Journal of Personality and Social Psychology.

It seems self-evident that our beliefs can strongly influence our behaviours and actions.

The well-worn adage, "if you believe you can or if you believe you can't, you're right", seems to have good science to back it up.

In a different study[5] published in the same journal in 2021, it was suggested that beliefs were the driver behind action.

If people believed their coping strategies for dealing with stress would be effective, it became effective.

If they didn't believe the strategy would be effective, then surprise, surprise, it wasn't effective.

Both these studies point to the significant influence our beliefs have on our behaviours and actions, and that belief can actually be a self-fulfilling prophecy.

The more we generate it, the more likely we are to succeed and so it continues as a virtuous circle.

If your beliefs are currently happening 'by accident', they can be made to happen a lot more 'on purpose'.

Why Bother?

If you don't believe it has any possibility of working at all, why would you even bother getting started with a project?

---

[5] Reference: Maher, J. P., Dunton, G. F., & Penedo, F. J. (2021). The role of beliefs about coping effectiveness in the relationship between coping and stress. Personality and Individual Differences.

Or if the sense of belief is very weak then when you're confronted with a series of hard challenges, why would you put the effort in?

The creation of belief is too important a subject to be left to chance.

If left to chance, the time and energy and resources you're prepared to put in can easily diminish, when actually what the project needs is your finest, most dedicated efforts to crack a hard problem.

If it really is one of the key differences between success and failure, then surely, you want to maximise the probability of absolute faith in your goal.

Big Bold Leaders

Marc Lore is a successful leader who exudes a Big Bold Mindset with a string of successful ventures to his name.

Perhaps best known for co-founding Jet.com, an online retailer that went head-to-head with Amazon, before being sold to Walmart for $3.3 billion.

In an interview with Inc. magazine, Lore said he believes "nothing is impossible" and that he is always looking for ways to disrupt established industries and create new markets.

Lore's view on impossible-sounding ventures is that they are often the most promising opportunities.

Lore believes when he is presented with a seemingly impossible challenge, he gets excited because he believes it is an opportunity to create something truly innovative and groundbreaking.

Lore is an advocate of going back to first principles.

The approach that looks at what has to be true in order for success to happen.

It's about focusing on what are the core things that need to happen.

To do this involves breaking down complex problems into fundamental components or 'first principles' and then reconstructing them from the ground up to arrive at a unique solution.

The approach is based on the idea that by understanding the fundamental principles underlying a problem, one can arrive at a more creative and effective solution.

What's the Probability of Success?

Lore looks at new projects and evaluates the probability of success.

An observation he makes is that if something only has a 20% chance of success, many leaders will shy away from it in search of something that perhaps has a 50% chance or better of succeeding.

Here's the thing though.

The opportunity with the 20% chance of success might carry a potential 100x return.

What would you rather do?

Place a series of smaller bets on opportunities with a 20% chance of success and a potential 100x return?

Or to go after more certain opportunities with a 50% plus probability of success but a lower return?

By definition, the Big Bold Mindset is about looking for the big opportunities and finding ways to bring those to life while quickly finding ways to experiment and rapidly iterate to what works.

Belief Construction in Progress

The deliberate construction of belief is something that anyone looking to develop a bigger bolder mindset should pay attention to.

Here's a selection of ideas for you to use and explore to see what works best for you:

Imagine the Future

Emily Balcetis, Associate Professor of Psychology at New York University is an advocate of Visualisation, of seeing and imagining the future.

Drawing on her research studying successful leaders in sport and business, she talks about the difference between Narrow and Broad Focus.

Balcetis draws a parallel with running a marathon.

At the start of a race, one's focus is broad and looking all around.

As you get further into the race, one's focus narrows so that you are just looking at the shorts of the runner in front of you that you want to overtake.

It's this very clear shift in focus from broad to narrow that helps gain perspective.

It's about breaking down the journey into smaller bite sized chunks rather than just seeing the global picture which helps to make the goal seem more achievable.

Step by step.

Create Momentum

Celebrate small wins and lock in the good feeling of making progress together as a team.

Creating a winning feeling which is shared amongst a team can create momentum and be a powerful accelerator.

Refuel Your Drive

In the last chapter, we explored WHY your goal matters.

Regularly revisiting this to reaffirm your mission is a powerful tool to regain perspective as is reminding oneself of the 'first principles' notions on which your ideas are built.

In the depths of moving forward, it can be easy to get lost in the weeds and taking time to gain perspective again will help.

Lift your head from the Present and remind yourself of the Future.

Get Uncomfortable

It's a truism that if you do what you've always done, you will get what you've always got. Actually, in a rapidly moving world, it could be worse than that if you do what you've always done!

To fuel the belief that you can be a challenger and tackle impossible obstacles, then it helps to do things on a regular basis that take you beyond your comfort zone.

The more you can get comfortable with being uncomfortable, the better chance you have.

Own It

Take ownership of your belief system.

It's more malleable than you might think and it's absolutely under your control.

Do not fall into the trap of just letting your belief structures happen by accident.

Start by reflecting on your own experiences and notice what has worked for you in the past to build your belief.

Make notes and find ways to deploy these ideas and techniques to projects you are working on today.

Your psychological profile and your relationship with what you believe is possible may become the single most important factor in how you can develop a bigger, bolder mindset.

Take control of this vital skill to sharpen your bigger bolder mindset.

Theme 2: Leading Bigger

Can you think of a time when you were in the zone?

When things happened effortlessly?

When the ideas, words and actions just flowed.

When you were hugely productive.

It feels good doesn't it, when we are in that zone of brilliance.

It's the state of mind that enables us to achieve our Big Bold Goals.

Here's the crux of this: should we wait for this state of mind to arrive or can we specifically, deliberately and consciously create that state of mind.

If you could be in that flow state twice as much are you now, how much more could you achieve?

My experience has shown me that when we lead ourselves effectively, we can create that optimal state.

The next four chapters will show you how.

Use them to lead yourself and be in the best state possible to achieve your Big Bold Goals.

Let them help you lead bigger.

Chapter 5 – Diversify Your Influence

"I really struggle being around some people, I find them draining."

"I feel really inspired being around some people, I love how we work together to solve hard problems."

Two different ends of the spectrum.

One challenging and the other uplifting.

Which people have an impact on you?

Positively or negatively?

In the same way as we can take control of what we believe, we can also take control of what and who we allow to influence us.

Paying attention to our influences can be a huge catalyst for our belief systems.

If we're surrounded by people with a mindset we aspire to, we cannot help but be influenced and start to adopt that way of thinking.

What I've noticed of the people who have mastered the Big Bold Mindset is that they are actively aware of the impact of the environments they operate within and take conscious control of who and what they allow into their lives.

What You See Is All There Is

You're going to be influenced by a variety of different things.

Who is controlling your access to those influences?

You or someone else?

Psychologist Daniel Kahneman coined the phrase *"what you see is all there is".*

Kahneman argues the human mind tends to rely almost exclusively on the information that is immediately available to it, as opposed to considering *all* relevant information.

According to Kahneman, the way that people make decisions is heavily influenced by the information that is currently in their conscious awareness, and they often fail to consider important details that are not immediately visible or salient.

If much of decision-making is reliant on what's around us, doesn't it make sense to pay attention to what else is around us and what's changing, so that we can make better decisions?

Where Are You?

When was the last time that you took some time to consciously audit what's shaping your world?

Here's a simple scoring system.

On a sheet of paper, draw out three columns, one as Positive, one as Neutral, and one as Negative.

Now, I want you to bring to mind a person who you feel has influence over your life or thoughts in some way.

Don't overthink it.

Do they lift you up?

Then write their name in the Positive column.

Leave you the same?

Then they'll go in the Neutral column.

Or leave you worse off?

Then they'll go in the Negative column

I want you to use this tool to write out all areas of your life where you can be influenced and rate those areas, people, practices by which column they sit in.

Try starting off with people.

List out 10 people who spring to mind either at work or at home.

Probably those you see most often.

Audit their influence and impact.

Next, move on to social media.

Who or what regularly appears in your feeds?

What about your physical environment?

What's on the walls around you or in your line of sight every day?

Think of how you choose to inform and entertain yourself, books, TV, magazines, movies.

What are you consuming regularly and how is it influencing you?

Start by paying attention to what influences already exist in your life.

Then, consider running some experiments to see if you can either dial up or dial down the positive or negative influences in your life.

It's important also to mention at this point the notion of diversity.

We can find ourselves living in our own echo chambers, in an increasingly polarised world.

Consider how much diversity of influence you currently have.

It's with this in mind that the influences you curate should absolutely include people with different views to your own so you are exposed to a wide range of ideas.

The distinction between views that challenge and make you think, versus negative and unhelpful ideas that take you away from your goals, is a very important one.

Don't throw the baby out with the bathwater.

Make sure you have exposure to a diverse range of ideas!

The Science of Influence

You've likely heard the saying that we are an average of the five people we spend most time with. That our growth is limited by the people we choose to surround ourselves with.

Is there truth in this wisdom? Is there robust science behind this philosophy?

In a study[6] published in the Journal of Business and Psychology in 2020, researchers surveyed CEOs who participated in mastermind groups.

The results were clear: being in a mastermind positively impacted business performance.

Leaders also reported higher levels of social support, learning, and personal growth compared to CEOs who did not participate in such groups.

Choosing social relationships with individuals who exhibit certain personality traits has a significant impact on our own behaviours and well-being.

In a 2021 study[7] published in the Journal of Business and Psychology, one team examined the impact of co-worker relationships on work outcomes.

They found that employees who had more positive relationships with their co-workers reported higher levels of job satisfaction, engagement, and performance.

---

6 Zenger, J. H., & Folkman, J. (2020). The impact of peer advisory groups on CEOs' social support, learning, and personal growth. Journal of Business and Psychology

7 The impact of coworker relationships on work outcomes: A meta-analytic review and future research agenda by Michael Tews, Jeongyun Kim, Sean Way, and Junchao (Jason) Wang. Publication: Journal of Business and Psychology, 2021.

The study also found that negative relationships with co-workers were associated with lower levels of these outcomes.

The science correlates with popular wisdom. We become more like the people we spend the most time with.

Unhealthy Thoughts

I'm fascinated by learning through extremes.

The extreme of anything shines a very bright spotlight on what is going on.

It's much easier to spot a pattern when something is under pressure.

When we make only small changes, it's much harder to see the impact.

Fast pattern spotting means you can learn and evolve that much faster.

Several years ago, I binge watched all five seasons of Breaking Bad over roughly the space of a couple of weeks (it's not something I recommend).

For the next couple weeks I couldn't work out why I felt dark and angry.

Of course, with hindsight, it was obvious that being heavily exposed to a dark drama series had a corrosive effect on my mental health.

Would I have noticed that if I'd watched a couple of episodes a week?

Probably not, but it would have still likely had a corrosive influence.

By being extreme, the influence became glaringly obvious.

How many influences are sitting just beneath your conscious awareness that are hindering your progress to your goals?

Is it a few or is it a lot?

Wouldn't you want to become aware of those influences?

When you notice what your precious attention is drawn to can help you make some better choices around where you direct it.

Big Bold Leaders

Being routinely exposed to curious bright minds is a good thing for accelerating a Big Bold Mindset.

Keeping the company of others grappling with hard challenges can inspire and provoke fresh thinking.

As the saying goes, steel sharpens steel.

The reverse is also true so be mindful of who you spend time with.

Mastermind groups bring together small groups of like-minded people to share challenges and ideas.

People who want to learn, support, and lift each other up.

I can't think of a single successful leader, who exhibits a Big Bold Mindset, who isn't actively involved in a mastermind group.

Melanie Perkins is the CEO of Canva, a business providing a graphic design platform.

In 2021, it was valued at $40 billion making it one of the most valuable privately held companies in the world.

Perkins is a member of the Entrepreneurs' Organization, a global peer-to-peer network of entrepreneurs, where she participates in a mastermind group with other CEOs.

In an interview with Forbes, Perkins described how the mastermind group provides her with valuable feedback and support.

She said, "It's very powerful to have a group of people who are not in your industry who can give you a different perspective and help you think outside the box".

In particular, the importance of being able to share challenges and successes with other entrepreneurs who understand what she's going through.

Melanie has credited much of Canva's success to the advice and guidance she has received from her network and for her, being part of a peer network is an essential part of being a successful leader.

Whether you work in a company, large or small, whether you are senior or junior, there are plenty of ways to get exposure to minds operating at a higher level.

For example, signing up for executive education run by a university, joining high-performer programmes, joining networks of like-minded people, book clubs, or even simply engaging with podcasts where people who aspire to emulate are interviewed.

The only caveat I would encourage is to make sure you are nowhere near being the smartest person in the room!

The more people around you who are performing at a higher level, the better.

Might it feel uncomfortable to start with?

Possibly, yes, but remember the notion of thinking bigger and bolder is about stepping beyond the comfort zone.

A Social Experiment

Social media offers great insight into what influence people allow themselves to consume.

Take Apple CEO Tim Cook as an example.

Look at who he follows on Twitter / X. Those 70[8] people didn't happen by accident. They have been carefully cultivated to give him a perspective on the world.

The same goes for the 217 people that Elon Musk follows.

And for the 124 people that Mary Barra, the CEO of General Motors follows.

---

[8] Follower numbers correct at the time of writing in April 2023

If you want to know what and why someone thinks the way they do, look at their influences.

Just studying the people they follow will tell you a huge amount about that person.

It's worth noting that these leaders aren't randomly filling their feeds with thousands of followers.

They have been carefully chosen.

Just have a look now at who you follow (on whatever social platforms you're active on).

What are those influences doing to you?

Are they the influences you want?

Want to think more like Tim Cook?

Unfollow everyone on your list and follow exactly the same people he does.

Want your Big Bold Mindset to be along the lines of anyone else?

Rinse, repeat.

Why not run an experiment and see how you get on?

You could even have two Twitter/X accounts. One that follows Big Bold Leaders and your current one. Switch between them for a week at a time and see what difference it makes.

You could get creative and choose a small handful of people who live the values and beliefs you aspire to. Find their influences and follow them to get a fresh hybrid view of the world based on their combined influences.

If the whole exercise raises nothing more than increased attention to better influences, I'd say that's worthwhile.

Cull the Crosses

Refer back to your influence audit.

Everything with a Cross. Can you remove all or nearly all of these influences?

Everything which is Neutral. Are there some things you can swap out to run some new experiments?

Everything which is Positive. Can you increase any of this?

This notion applies to everything in your world. Some ideas to consider:

Line of Sight

How do you want to feel when you wake up?

Put images in your line of sight that invoke that feeling.

For example in my immediate line of sight are two seascape photographs. For me personally, this immediately lifts me.

What images would lift you up?

Maybe you want to be thoughtful, so a thought-provoking quote or reminder?

Think about what feeling you want to invoke and choose wisely.

Pictures, objects, books and so on.

Repeat for each room in the house.

In our kitchen where we spend most of our time as a family, we have a large painting we created with the words “We Are Learners” and images the family created of different ways we learn,

Follow this process with all the aspects from the influence audit. What you read, what or who you follow. Your morning and evening routines. Spending a bit less time with people who pull you down and more with those who lift you up. Try a new podcast?

The list of experiments is myriad.

The results can be impactful.

Don’t be asleep at the wheel and leave it to chance.

This is under your control.

Under Control

In 2000, I was one of a crew of 18 people racing competitively around the world.

Twelve of us were core crew who raced the entire globe.

The remaining six places were up for grabs for ‘leggers’ who did one or two of the seven different stages of the race.

It was distinctly noticeable to see the impact of each legger crew change.

Life was intensely magnified as we lived at the extremes of the harshest weather conditions on the planet with hurricanes, 100-foot waves and icebergs.

Each person brought a very different vibe, which had a noticeable impact.

Driven focused leggers brought extra concentration on results.

Kind thoughtful leggers brought a gentler touch.

Comedians brought more humour.

The choice of crew was not under our control.

Leggers were allocated by race organisers and we had to quickly learn to adapt and welcome in new people and help them to play their part in our team.

In that environment each person shaped their own world.

Who they spent most time with. What they read. What they listened to. What they focused on. What they paid attention to. This is about taking control.

If you want a Big Bold Mindset, deliberately, specifically, and consciously curate your influences.

This something 100% under your control and could quite simply be the most impactful thing you can do to shape your bigger bolder mindset.

Chapter 6 – Construct Your Identity

"There's no way I can do that. I'm not that type of person. That's just not me".

Have you ever said words like this?

I certainly have and that has led to many missed opportunities because I had taken ownership of a limiting story of who I was.

It's often easier to see it in others than it is in ourselves.

Can you think of anyone you know who is very capable but they talk themselves out of doing things because of a story they hold?

If we can see it in others, perhaps others can see what we can't see in ourselves?

I currently spend much of my working life standing on stages speaking to senior leaders at world leading companies.

Roll back a few decades to my school days and I could have been voted "least likely to present on stage".

Perhaps you too have a similar story?

Something that was once unimaginable and then sometime later came to pass.

So what changed?

Who chose the current story of who you are?

Did it happen by accident or did you choose it?

What Self Will You Be Today?

In the film *Darkest Hour,* Winston Churchill has received the telegram to call him to the palace to meet the King to be appointed Prime Minister.

As he prepares to take the mantle for his greatest challenge yet, he stands in front of his hat rack and asks himself the question: "Which self shall I be today?" and then selects the appropriate hat and walks out of the door.

It's a revealing moment.

It's a moment in which he shows the power of having different identities.

Identities and stories that we can use to empower us in different scenarios.

These things don't happen by accident.

They are as a result of thinking through the different parts of your life and who you need to be in each different situation.

It's worth reflecting on.

For the different roles you play in your life, who do you need to show up as?

At work, at home, with friends.

What do you need to do to change your perspective?

Where Are You?

Take a pen and paper and sketch out what words come to mind.

What is the current story you carry of who you are?

Do you show up in different ways in different situations?

Do you have different 'selves' that you can call upon at will?

Who chooses which 'self' shows up in different situations?

Think of the self you are with your partner and family, the one you are with your team, the one you are with board members, the one you are with friends, the one you are when you play sport.

Once you have captured your current self in each main environment in your life, take a moment to pause and reflect.

Are you happy with the self who shows up at different times?

There is work we can do to evolve one's internal story, your internal dialogue.

The Science of Identity

The phrase psychologists use around this mindset of choosing how to show up is *Identity Flexibility.*

A paper published in the Journal of Personality and Social Psychology[9] found that our self-identity can be flexible and adaptable.

Identity flexibility refers to our ability to adjust, adapt, or modify our self-concept, beliefs, values, and behaviours in response to different social contexts or situations.

The concept recognises that we possess multiple aspects of our identity and that these aspects can be expressed or emphasised differently depending on the environment.

The findings were that people with a more flexible self-identity were better able to cope with life changes and were less likely to experience negative psychological outcomes such as anxiety and depression.

It's a skill set we can't afford to not have.

A recent report by McKinsey estimated that up to 800 million jobs globally will be displaced by AI by 2030.

This trend is accelerating, not decreasing.

One of the core skill sets that will help people transition is that of reinvention.

How many people do you know who define their identity by the role that they do?

I'm an accountant, I'm a programmer, I'm a writer and so on.

---

[9] Identity flexibility during adulthood: Perspectives on multidimensionality and plasticity in self-definition, Dorthe Kirkegaard Thomsen, Sarah E. Gaede, and Steen Kaargaard Nielsen. Published in Journal of Personality and Social Psychology, Volume: 11, Year: 2018

What happens when what you identify with gets done better by a machine?

Where does that leave your identity?

I truly believe that one of the most important skill sets that any of us can master is that of reinvention, of redefining who we are and how we bring value to the world and others.

What happens if you are unwilling or unable to redefine your identity and re-calibrate your compass?

It's a recipe for running aground much in the same way as the ships navigating by the charts created by Captain Cook several hundred years ago.

Big Bold Leaders

Arnold Schwarzenegger, the Austrian American actor, bodybuilder, and politician, is an unlikely and interesting example of someone who has reinvented himself numerous times throughout their career.

He has consistently transformed himself throughout his life, achieving success in various fields.

Schwarzenegger's initial claim to fame was as a professional bodybuilder. He became a dominant force in the sport, winning the prestigious Mr. Olympia contest multiple times. His dedication to bodybuilding helped establish his image as an icon in the fitness industry.

However, Schwarzenegger didn't stop at bodybuilding. He transitioned into acting in the 1970s, initially facing scepticism due to his thick Austrian accent and imposing physique.

He persevered, starring in iconic roles such as the Terminator in the "Terminator" film series, which catapulted him to international stardom. He successfully balanced action and comedy genres in his acting career, showcasing his versatility.

In addition to acting, Schwarzenegger ventured into entrepreneurship, notably investing in real estate and opening a chain of fitness centres. His business acumen reinforced his ability to reinvent himself.

One of his most notable and unexpected reinventions came when he entered politics. Schwarzenegger ran for and was elected as the Governor of California, serving from 2003 to 2011. His political journey demonstrated adaptability and the ability to navigate complex political landscapes.

After his political career, Schwarzenegger continued to be a public figure, using his platform to advocate for various causes, including environmental issues and fitness awareness.

His story is a testament to the power of reinvention. He transformed from a bodybuilder to a Hollywood superstar, ventured into business, successfully entered politics, and maintained a prominent public role advocating for issues close to his heart. His story inspires individuals to embrace change and continuously reinvent themselves to achieve lasting success in various pursuits.

He is someone who absolutely exemplifies the Big Bold Mindset and is unafraid to innovate and try new things.

How to Flex

You can harness your identity flexibility and here are some tools to help you do that.

A Who List

Plenty of us start a fresh week with a To Do List.

Not many people start with a WHO list, as in who will you be this week, how will you show up?

Look at what's coming up in your calendar.

Who do you need to be for each different situation?

Imagine some different scenarios:

- A new sales call
- A tricky negotiation
- An employee appraisal
- A call with a potential partner
- A mastermind meeting with your peers
- Supper with your husband/ wife/ partner
- A call with your lawyers

Just take a moment to reflect on the ideal outcome for the call and which self of yours would best serve you? Chances are they are very different selves.

Maybe go through each appointment and consider which part of you needs to show up. The empathetic person, the negotiator, with humility, with energy to sell a vision? You get the idea.

Make a note to ask which self needs to step forward.

Some leaders I know go further and have different names for their different selves that they can call upon. Who will you be? Who do you need to be?

Script it Out

Many years ago as an entrepreneur, I knew I was not the leader that I wanted to be.

I reflected deeply on this and having spent time studying a wide selection of impressive business pioneers, I was ready to redefine my leadership style.

It started with a script.

I literally wrote out a script for how I wanted to show up as a leader.

What my daily routines would be, how I would handle difficult situations, how I would make decisions and how I wanted to guide my team.

My ideas were fuelled by the stories and actions of others, and in my script, I imagined how I wanted to show up.

Each time as I've reinvented myself, I've shaped a new script.

What's the script you need to lead in times of exponential change?

How different is it from what you do today?

How different is what you have done in the past?

Visualise Reality

Inspired by the work of Professor Maxwell Maltz, many years ago I adopted a visualisation technique called the Theatre of the Mind.

Visualisation is a widely recognised technique to form words, pictures, and feelings in our minds.

It's long been used in sports and is commonly used by top athletes to improve their performance.

By visualising themselves successfully executing a particular technique or skill, athletes can enhance their muscle memory, build confidence, and reduce anxiety.

In the Theatre of your Mind, spend a few minutes every day with your eyes closed and imagine sitting in the front row of a cinema watching a film.

You are the lead character in the film and you are acting out the script you've written out by hand and you are successfully handling the situations as they arise.

You are taking your script and converting the words into pictures and feelings in your mind.

Take the time to notice the small details and really be present in the film.

Take the time to notice how you feel.

You're painting a picture into your mind of the story you want to bring to life which makes it more likely to come to life.

To delve deeper into this fascinating area, the work of Emily Balcetis, Associate Professor at NYU has much more to say on how visualisation can be practically applied and her book Clearer, Closer Better adds real nuance and depth to making visualisation work better.

Change with the Seasons

American Entrepreneur, Tom Bilyeu speaks regularly on the topic of entrepreneurship and the question of identity.

Tom has crafted his identity as being that of a Learner.

It is a very practical identity for all seasons.

Why?

Because if you are a learner and what you value yourself for is being a learner, then no matter what situation arises, you can always learn and figure out a way forward.

So long as the challenge you are facing does not defy the laws of physics, then it is highly likely that someone else has faced this challenge before and figured out the answer.

And if they have, then as a learner, you can too.

I can't think of a better identity to have than being that of a learner. It quite simply opens the door to growth and reinvention.

Deliberately Construct

"I wasn't this Kennedy guy. I carefully, deliberately, and consciously constructed him."

The words of Dan Kennedy, aka The Renegade Millionaire, and someone who truly understood the power of the flexible identity.

He created the persona that he needed to be successful in his chosen career.

The person with the Big Bold Mindset absolutely understands the power of the flexible identity and creates the time and space to craft and shape the internal story of who they need to be.
Who do you need to be for success in what you are doing?

What flexible identity could you construct?

Chapter 7 – Rewrite the Narrative

It was another day of going to work with the latest argument still ringing in my ears.

I was consumed by the rights and wrongs and the high-tide mark left by words that once spoken, can't be unspoken.

It was corrosive to my mental health.

It was corrosive to my ability to do my best work; to be able to achieve my best work that was needed to achieve our business goals.

The impact of conflict at home and a long string of unresolved arguments had left me in a dark place.

We had two young children and we weren't being the best parents we could be.

My business was struggling and I was working long hours.

As a couple, we definitely were not listening to each other, nor working as a team.

It was a toxic formula.

Something needed to change.

It appears we weren't alone.

In a YouGov survey of senior managers, over 69% of them admitted to significant problems in their private relationships while in their current role.

Is this the price of ambition?

Failed home life relationships?

Surely there has to be a better way.

I believe there is.

Write a Fresh Story

What is the story of your home life, your life outside work?

Perhaps you don't have one.

At the start of a relationship, the future looks exciting.

It's easy and it flows.

As the years progress, challenges arise.

Health, finance, career progression, parenting.

Multiple challenges which require teamwork to navigate these together.

How much time have you invested in thinking about how you work as a 'home team'?

None, some, a lot?

Can you think of a more exciting story of the future for your home team?

I truly believe that the power of deep listening, of co-creating a powerful shared story of the future is the single most important thing that anyone can do to improve one's home life.

Through creating a shared story of the future, you're setting expectations around what you can create together.

And all too often, while doing this, we look to the past with remorse around what once was, rather than looking forward to what could be.

There are two huge benefits to choosing the latter.

First, anchoring around an exciting, shared story of the future is more likely to create a strong stable supportive base at home, which can enable you to show up in the best way possible.

Second, the skills and the process needed to co-create the exciting, shared story is one of the most powerful leadership skills you can develop.

Where Are You?

If you are in a relationship, do you have an exciting shared co-created story of the future?

If you aren't in a relationship, could you imagine using these ideas in a future relationship? Could they have helped in a past relationship? What can you learn from this?

It may be that these ideas might not work for you, but what have you got to lose?

The opportunity is to take your relationship to another more exciting level, to create a supportive stable base and to develop a highly valuable set of skills.

A set of skills that are crucial to the Big Bold Mindset.

The Science of Support

A study by the University of Georgia[10] found that people with supportive spouses had more job satisfaction, were more likely to stay in their job, and were less likely to experience burnout.

A supportive spouse can provide emotional support and serve as a sounding board for work-related issues.

Specifically, in the context of pursuing ambitious goals, a study published in the Journal of Personality and Social Psychology[11] found that individuals who received emotional support from their close relationships were more likely to achieve their goals than those who didn't.

In the study, participants were randomly assigned to receive either emotional support or no support from their significant other while pursuing a personal goal.

Participants were asked to report on their goal pursuit progress and their perceived support from their significant other at several points throughout the study.

Perhaps unsurprisingly, participants who received emotional support were more likely to achieve their goals and reported feeling more satisfied with their progress than those who did not receive support.

---

[10] Conducted by researchers at the University of Georgia and published in the Journal of Marriage and Family in 2017

[11] Published in the Journal of Personality and Social Psychology in 2010

Having supportive relationships can provide individuals with the encouragement and resources they need to overcome obstacles and achieve their goals.

Painfully Distracted

Anyone who's been through a painful relationship situation needs no reminder of the distraction it causes.

It's not good on any level:

It's corrosive to mental health.

It's corrosive to productivity.

It's corrosive to achieving big bold goals.

It's corrosive financially.

For the record, some relationships of course are not meant to be.

Relationships are complex things and I know of many people in difficult situations for which there are few easy answers.

Is what I am suggesting the silver bullet for everyone?

Absolutely not.

What works for someone might now work for someone else.

And of course, with relationships, it's complicated because there are two people with thoughts, feelings, and ideas, not one person.

All I would urge anyone to do is to consider developing the leadership skills to be able to craft that exciting story of the future using the tools in this chapter.

Perhaps it may not benefit you in your current situation, but skills acquired can be used at any time and remember these are universal skills that can be used at home or at work.

Big Bold Leaders

Reshma Saujani is the Founder and CEO of Girls Who Code.

It's a remarkable organisation on a mission to close the gender gap in technology by providing computer science education to young women.

Since its founding in 2012, Girls Who Code has reached over 500 million people through its programs, books, and media campaigns.

They have trained over 300,000 girls in coding and computer science skills, and 90% of Girls Who Code alumni have gone on to major or minor in computer science in college.

A Big Bold Mission indeed and Saujani is definitely someone who lives a Big Bold Mindset.

In an interview with CNBC, Saujani talked about the importance of work-life integration rather than work-life balance.

She emphasised the need to prioritise one's mental health and personal life in order to perform at one's best.

She, like a new generation of leaders, recognises the importance of having a strong home life in order to be successful in their work.

They prioritise their mental health, personal lives, and families, and believe that doing so allows them to be more effective and productive in their professional endeavours.

Deep Listening

Perhaps the simplest and yet the most impactful tool I've ever developed is that of Deep Listening.

This is not to be confused with Active Listening.

Active Listening involves paying full attention to the speaker, both verbally and non-verbally, in order to understand their message.

The speaker gets the confirmation their point is coming across and listeners absorb more content and understanding by being consciously engaged.

Active Listening is about listening only.

Deep Listening is the process of both Listening and Creating. Together.

Deep Listening is a very specific process I developed to create a fresh story of the future between two or more people.

I originally created this for use at home and then developed it for use at work as the technique is equally applicable there.

It follows these steps (described from the point of view of two people):

Step 1 - *The Open Searching Question*

It all starts with one searching open question.

In a home context, a favourite of mine is "what is truly important to you in life?"

In a work context, I like questions along the lines of: "what would make you feel proud if we could achieve it together?".

Questions that are anchored in feelings.

Each person, with pen and paper, spends time writing their answers to this question.

Take as long as you need.

When you get stuck and stop writing, ask the question again and see what else comes up.

Continue until you have nothing left to add.

Step 2 - *One Person Gets Seen, Heard and Understood*

One person shares. One person listens.

With blank fresh sheets, Person A asks Person B the open searching question.

As Person B shares what is on their list, Person A writes down everything they say.

They just listen and write.

When Person B gets to the end of the list, Person A asks if there is anything else.

Invariably there is and new things get added.

Person A writes them all down.

Person A then asks again if there is anything else.

They only stop when B gets to the end of their thoughts.

No comments. No additional words. No added views.

Just listening and being 100% present to everything they say.

The playback can then begin.

Person A says I'd like to share with you what I just heard.

And then replays everything they have heard. Verbatim.

At the end of the playback, A asks B if they heard them correctly.

Invariably, new ideas, edits, additional explanations will arise.

A writes all these down too and repeats the playback.

The playback only stops when B says "Yes, you have understood me correctly'.

This exercise on its own is such a powerful activity.

In the thousands of times we have had this done at workshops and events, it always returns the same reaction.

There is something magical about a person being 100% seen, heard, understood, and listened to.

If you do nothing else with this book other than take one idea, I would invite you to consider it to be this one.

It is the most human thing for any of us to be seen, heard and understood. It is the magic which lights people up.

Step 3 - The Other Person Gets Seen, Heard and Understood

Step 3 is simple to describe.

It's Step 2 but A and B swapping.

Step 3 only stops when A says "Yes, you have understood me correctly'.

Step 4 - Where The Magic Happens

This is where the process goes way beyond listening.

This is where you get to create.

Both A and B now have a sheet of paper of what is important to each other.

With only those sheets in front of you, with a highlighter, look for what you share in common.

It's really important that you only flag the areas you share.

Not the things that are important to one person and not the other.

Genuinely only the shared items.

There might only be a very small number of things.

That's ok.

Take these shared items and put them on a clean sheet of paper.

These are the Lego building blocks, the foundational elements of your new story.

S*tep 5 - Get Creative and Have Fun*

It's now down to you together to co-create an exciting story of the future using only those elements that you share in common.

How can you construct something completely new built on something where you both feel listened to and where you are both fully engaged because it is important to both of you?

It's really hard to build on conflict. Where one party wants one thing and the other wants something else.

It's much easier to build, to create when you are aligned and creating something that doesn't yet exist.

This process could take a few hours. It could be done over a few weeks and when we first did this as a couple, we took around three months.

It's developing powerful skills that can be used to engage any team. At home or at work.

And finally, if you might be wondering about whether you and your partner will share anything in common, I have something to share.

This concern is the most common one I've heard in the thousands of times I have done this.

And I have never seen it happen.

People always find some things in common.

Things that may have been forgotten about long ago in the past, buried under the detritus of day-to-day life.

There is magic in rediscovering those forgotten dreams, ambitions, and stories.

Focus on the life in front of you. Not the challenges behind you.

Step 6 - Get Focused on the Shared Story

As you shape the story, make it visible to keep it front of mind.

Filed away in a drawer gathering dust won't cut the mustard.

Remember, what you see is all there is.

Figure out ways to grapple with the challenge, the shared story and how you can bring it to life.

Use the ideas in this book to bring your story to life.

Your Chart to the Future

The Big Bold Mindset by definition is ambitious.

Hungry and wanting more.

There is an oft unspoken rule that the price of work success is personal relationships.

We've heard the stories of the successful leaders with a string of failed marriages.

I reject the idea that it *has* to be that way.

When my wife and I created our story, I still worked crazy long hours, but we were aligned and working in harmony towards an important shared goal.

Not one that was mine and mine alone.

This is why this process is priceless. It's about creating that shared story together, something that both parties buy into.

At home as it is at work.

How much more would you give if you felt listened to, understood, and had a hand in shaping the future of where you are going as a team?

Wouldn't you feel more engaged?

Outdated charts of how we are meant to be, risk sending relationships onto the rocks.

Use a new chart and develop the Deep Listening skills to create your shared story of the future.

Chapter 8 – Direct Your Attention

I've no idea where the time went.

I went to my phone to find the address for where I'm going this afternoon and emerged 45 minutes later.

Let me check the time of my morning meeting and if it's Zoom or Teams.

Shit. I forgot to cancel that other meeting.

Didn't someone message me last night and I've got a mental note to get back to them?

Oh that's an interesting news alert.

Ever get distracted because you've got so many communication channels open all the time?

So many information feeds.

Lots and lots of nudges and interruptions that decimate your focus and productivity.

The constant ping notifications alerting you to a new snippet of information.

Another dopamine hit.

Is this you?

Is this someone you know?

This could quite easily be the single most corrosive thing of our generation.

The continual hijacking of our mental faculties.

Be honest.

How much time gets lost in a vortex of pointless information that you never knew you needed to know?

This is a real and pressing problem of our time.

It's not getting any better.

You know this already, of course.

You will see immediately that reclaiming this stolen time is crucial for the Big Bold Mindset.

According to Insider Intelligence[12], in 2022, the average time spent on mobile devices is over 4.5 hours per day.

That's 31.5 hours a week!

How much progress on your Big Bold Goals could you make if you reclaimed 31.5 hours a week?

If only we could consistently reclaim our time and focus.

We're all familiar with the problem.

Solutions can be a bit trickier. Full self-disclosure: This is something I still battle with

---

12 https://www.insiderintelligence.com/insights/us-time-spent-with-media/

Setting Intention

Let me tell you a story.

For two years as we sailed the world, we were literally unplugged for weeks and months at a time.

We talked more.

We played games.

We sat around the dinner table together.

We connected more as humans.

We got to know each other.

We were off the grid. Disconnected from the minute-by-minute barrage on our senses from Email, Facebook, Instagram, Twitter, LinkedIn, YouTube, Netflix and so on.

The year after we returned was a blitz of re-connection. Smartphones, iPads, Emails, social media, and Netflix became the standard.

We were immediately immersed back to a digital world.

A year later, we set to sea again for six weeks.

We disconnected.

The magic returned.

The dinner table conversations, the playing, the reading, the human connection. There was more laughter. More time knowing who we were as humans. It was stark.

We'd gone from one extreme to another and back again.

Back home again, the devices returned.

It revealed just how corrosive the "always connected" lifestyle is.

To have a Big Bold Mindset is to be self-aware of where your time and focus is going.

I wonder how many of us are asleep at the wheel and slowly over time, our time and attention has been stolen by clever technology designers from Silicon Valley hijacking your psychology.

This is your, and my reminder to take back control.

Where Are You?

How much deep focused work do you do in a day? In a week?

How much time do you spend on your smartphone?

On social media platforms?

On email?

It's a formidable foe. Especially as it's been cleverly interwoven into the most revolutionary productivity device known to us.

And in equal measure, the most revolutionary yet zero-productive device known to us.

Yes, our smartphones. A double-edged sword if ever there was one.

31.5 hours a week. Are you higher or lower?

Would you like to reclaim time and focus?

The Science of Attention

The research on the impact of excessive device usage and time on social media only points in one direction.

Unsurprisingly, it's not good news.

Excessive use of it is making us dumber.

One study[13] found that excessive use of social media is associated with decreased grey matter volume in the amygdala and insula regions of the brain, which are involved in emotional regulation and decision making.

In another study[14], excessive social media was found to be associated with decreased attention span and poorer performance on cognitive tasks.

These are not isolated research findings.

There will almost certainly be many more insights as more research continues.

Don't expect the results to start pointing in a different direction.

How much of these insights come as a surprise?

---

13 Liu, X., Hu, Y., & Chen, J. (2021). Exploring the relationship between social media addiction and gray matter volume in a sample of Chinese college students. Addictive Behaviors, 113, 106695.
14 Kılıç, E., & Samur, Y. (2020). The relationship between social media use and attention performance: An investigation of the mediating role of fear of missing out. Computers in Human Behavior, 105, 106213.

How much work are you doing to actively counteract this. For you? For your family?

In the Netflix Documentary, The Social Dilemma, leading executives at social media companies reveal that they strictly control or remove access to their kids on social media platforms.

Do you need any more convincing that something has to be done to regain our ability to function with full cognitive ability?

It's affecting our mental health.

Johann Hari writes in Stolen Focus about how the rise of technology, especially social media, is leading to an epidemic of attention problems, loneliness, and specifically, anxiety.

Social media and smartphones are designed to keep us hooked, leading to a constant need for attention and validation.

The use of technology has led to an increase in anxiety and depression, as people compare their lives to others, online, and feel inadequate.

The rise of social media has led to a decline in face-to-face communication, leading to an increase in loneliness and isolation.

Addressing this challenge is broader than simply shaping our Big Bold Mindset. It's about how we take care of our mental health. For us, for our families, for our friends, for our teams.

Unchecked, this will present a serious challenge to you achieving your big bold goals and the mindset you need to achieve it

Big Bold Leaders

Indicative of the widely recognized size of the challenge, many successful leaders have opinions on what works for them.

Here's a selection of ideas:

Create a 'phone bed' outside of the bedroom to avoid the temptation of using smartphones at night and first thing in the morning - Arianna Huffington, founder of the Huffington Post

Set boundaries and disconnect from devices to maintain work-life balance, particularly during periods of stress or intense workload - Ursula von der Leyen, President of the European Commission.

Take breaks from technology to recharge and focus on self-care, including meditation, journaling, or exercise - Indya Moore, actor and model.

A quick google search also reveals a host of similar sounding advice such as:

Turn off push notifications and set specific times during the day to check messages and emails.

Set priorities and focus on high-priority tasks before checking emails or using social media.

Have you tried any of these ideas before?

Did they work?

Ideas like this sound good, but do they really work? A small number of successful leaders have publicly shared their struggles with internet addiction and their strategies for overcoming it.

Chris Anderson, founder of TED, has written about his experience with internet addiction and how he used ideas like setting boundaries, such as setting specific times for email and social media usage.

The phrase Screen Dependency Disorder[15] has become a term to describe the challenge we face.

One of the executives profiled in The Social Dilemma is Tristan Harris. A former Google design ethicist and founder of the Center for Humane Technology. His work explores the influences that hijack human attitudes, behaviours, and beliefs.

Specifically, he studies how major technology platforms wield dangerous power over our ability to make sense of the world and is a vocal advocate for addressing internet addiction and promoting healthier technology use through design.

The challenge is real and ongoing.

While Harris and others may create change in the platforms we use, it's up to us to shape the best strategies we can to reclaim focus and attention.

The Deep Work Checklist

Creativity is the connection of two previously unrelated ideas. I'd like to offer you the product of two ideas which I've found useful.

The source of the ideas were two books:

One is *Deep Work* by Cal Newport - the focus of which is how we can train ourselves to work deeply absent of distraction.

---

[15] https://www.hibamagazine.com/screen-dependency-disorder/

The other is *The Checklist Manifesto* by Atul Gwande. As a Medical Doctor he shares how many lives have been saved by developing checklists. Deceptively simple, yet powerful and life changing.

The Deep Work Checklist was the simple evolution of the two ideas.

The goal is a distraction free state to do your best work.

The strategy is a checklist to tick off each day focused on the most salient reminders for you.

Remember "what you see is all there is"?

This is that sentiment on a visible sheet of paper to nudge you to do your best work.

Some ideas that you might found helpful:

- Reminders to switch off smartphones and distraction.
- Use a paper diary to block-time the day.
- Focus on the most important goal for that day/ week/ month.
- Work on your rituals/ habits
- Regularly take breaks outside in nature
- Take time to think and reflect on your hardest challenges.
- Shut down procedures at the end of the day to transition to home life.

As an ambitious leader, I'm certain you will have your own views and ideas on what you have found works and doesn't work for you.

If you'd like my checklist, I'm very happy to share it with you to prompt more ideas. Connect with me on LinkedIn, I'm easy to find, and ask me to send it to you.

Get Focused

How is your ability to focus and do deep work?

Does it come easily or do you need to work hard at it?

The ideas shared in this chapter focus on the cognitive aspects. Things that you can specifically do to improve your ability to focus.

There's a part of this which is beyond cognitive. The reason the social media companies are successful is because designers understand the inner workings of our psychology.

The reasons we do things. At a chemical level, we become addicted to the dopamine hits of another 'like', a new piece of information, and so on.

I'm no clinical psychologist but I'd be amazed if any work one does beyond a cognitive level, doesn't start to help with any ability to handle our propensity to be distracted.

In Chapter 21, you will find some ideas and experiments to adventure beyond the cognitive and to go deeper into understanding your own psychology.

The invitation is to run some experiments around this and explore your own need for stimulation which can be the reason why one can become so easily distracted.

The nature of the Big Bold Mindset is to be open and consider possibilities.

Possibilities which most others dismiss as being ridiculous.

In an area where experts don't appear to have a convincing solution, I invite you to explore all avenues.

Theme 3: Bigger Together

Have you ever taken on a big challenge and tried to do it on your own?

Tricky isn't it!

I'd go further and say impossible.

At the heart of the Big Bold Mindset is figuring out the skills to engage a team of people and harness the unique and diverse skill sets and ideas that every Big Bold Goal demands.

We only ever get to be bigger together, not alone.

You've got to master the skills of understanding humans and how to engage others to join the journey.

The next four chapters will show you how.

Use them to unleash the extraordinary talents and potential for you and your team.

Let them help you become bigger together.

Chapter 9 – Put People First

We were all over the front-page headlines.

The humiliation was very public.

Internally there were arguments, divisions and factions forming.

It was gut wrenching.

Was this the end of the journey that we had all put so much into?

Was it the end of our dream?

We had crashed our boat.

It wasn't a small crash.

In front of a spectator-packed Wellington harbour watched by thousands of people, we had sailed our 50-tonne boat at full speed into the side of Save The Children, one of the 11 other boats we were racing round the world with.

The recriminations carried on for days and culminated in our Captain resigning within the week.

As one of the two watch-leaders, I shared the responsibility for our very public failure.

How could we have got it so wrong?

How could we have gone from being winners to failures?

We had won the first leg racing from the UK to America.

We had been the first boat to round Cape Horn, and at the start of racing from New Zealand to Australia, we were placed third overall in the fleet.

And now it had all gone up in flames.

What happened to us?

Focused on the Wrong Thing

Our crew were ordinary people.

Many of whom had no sailing experience and who had signed up for an extraordinary experience to race round the world as an amateur crew over a period of 10 months.

In January 2000, eight months before we would set sail from Southampton on the south coast of the UK, the several hundred crew were divided into 12 different teams.

How each team developed and worked together would be the only thing that separated first place and last place.

This was not the story of elite athletes. This was the story of ordinary people taking on a big bold goal - a seemingly impossible challenge.

To win, we had to be fast.

Our team focus was boat speed.

How could we make the boat go faster than anyone else?

This became our sole focus as a team and we developed the mantra "A fast boat is a happy boat".

It perfectly matched the business logic of the day.

It perfectly matched the sporting logic of the day.

People became secondary to the numbers.

We, the crew, were the means to an end rather than the end in itself.

By the time we were halfway around the world, as a crew, we were burnt out. Feeling unappreciated, unheard. Exhausted.

All to pay the price of faster boat speed.

We became dysfunctional as a crew and when the pressure was on at the start of the race, we failed to respond as a team and crashed the boat.

The elite sporting analogy reached the end of the road.

Our race, much like business, was a marathon. Not a sprint.

We had been duped.

We'd believed all the mantras of the day:

"Will it make the boat go faster?"

"What are the numbers? Drive harder. Push more."

We, and all the prevailing advice, was the wrong way round.

It wasn't that a fast boat is a happy boat.

It was the opposite way around.

A happy boat is a fast boat.

A boat where people feel heard and seen.

A boat where people feel appreciated, where each person plays to their strengths.

Of course, we have to keep a focus on the numbers, in sailing and in business. What's important to remember, though, is that the numbers are the destination we aim for, the port we're headed to, but how the ship gets there, how its crew feel whilst getting there, dictates how competitive we can be.

I learnt the hard way that the numbers are the trailing indicator and that the people are the leading indicator.

When you put people first, the results will follow.

Where Are You?

Who was the best leader that you ever had?

Can you bring them to mind right now?

Were they the best leader because they only cared about the results?

Or were they the best leader because they cared about you? Because they took the time to listen to you, to guide you, to understand you? What made them brilliant in your opinion? Was it that they only focused on results? Or that they listened to the team to achieve them?

Leadership is not a title.

It's a mindset. It's about how you look after those around you. It's about how you show up.

How do you show up?

Is it like the best leader you have ever had? Is there room for improvement?

I think if we are all honest, we all have room to be better.

What conversation could you have with someone today to be 100% present and to think about what you can do to help them develop on their journey?

The Science of Performance

McKinsey & Company published research in 2021 after surveying over 1,200 business leaders and 6,000 employees across industries and regions.

The report, *The New Essentials of Employee Experience,* found that companies that prioritise employee well-being and engagement are more likely to outperform their peers in terms of financial performance.

Some key findings:

Companies that rank in the top quartile for employee experience are more than *twice* as likely to be in the top quartile for financial performance than companies in the bottom quartile.

Employee experience is a critical factor in attracting and retaining talent. Employees are more likely to stay with their current employer if they feel valued and supported.

Communication and feedback are key drivers of employee experience. Open and transparent communication from leaders, as well as opportunities to provide feedback and be heard, is crucial.

The findings are clear cut. Teams that look after people get better results. When you put people first, the results will follow.

It's All a Transaction

"*As a team, we are very transactional. We know we need to be more people focused, but we're not very good at getting there*".

"*Our culture has always been about performance and results*".

"*We have had quite a few people experience burnout*".

"*We have a number of people with mental health challenges*".

"*The culture is that no-one really feels safe to share what they are feeling*".

I lose track of how many conversations I have like this every month.

These are conversations with leaders who have demanding results that they need to achieve.

Conversations with leaders where the organisational culture has followed an outdated approach that prioritises numbers above people.

Cultures where the leaders have been duped.

Duped by elite-sporting models that are all about the sprint, not the marathon.

Duped by an outdated mentality that forgets that it is humans who drive results. Not the other way around.

It's the equivalent of steering your team using Captain Cook's charts.

The first step is to realise your team has an operating model past its sell-by date.

The second step is to begin that culture change journey.

Big Bold Leaders

In my work as a leadership speaker on the Big Bold Mindset, I get to spend time with some inspiring leaders.

One such leader is Rob Brien. Rob is the COO of an international manufacturing group in the metals sector. At the group's recent senior leadership event, I spent time with Rob and his team.

Their focus is on a triple bottom line. The three P's. People, Planet and Profits.

Their team recognise the crucial importance of people to be able to drive the business.

Their team recognise the responsibility their organisation has towards the planet and creating businesses that are environmentally sustainable with a positive impact.

And of course, there has to be profit in the mix because without it, no-one would have jobs and investors wouldn't back projects.

It's about achieving the right balance.

What is heartening with Rob and his team is that this is not just a slogan or green washing. In conversation with many of the 42 senior leaders, this is a very real concept that everyone has at the front of their minds.

Rob is a new generation of leaders who are not trapped by the dogma of past thinking and models. Leaders who are prepared to orient around the challenges of today and tomorrow. Leaders who genuinely care about the people they work and the communities and world we live in.

It's more than just the right thing to do.

It's actually the best thing for business too. In a world where social media brings transparency, talent and clients are migrating more than ever to organisations who care. Organisations like Rob's who put people and the planet front and centre alongside profit.

Putting People First

What does it mean in practice to put a people first approach into practice?

Here are some ideas that you can put into action immediately:

Notice the Small Details

Notice and let those around you know when they do something well. Especially the Unsung Heroes - the people who seldom get recognition. Be specific with what you share - be detailed and be kind.

I've yet to meet a person who doesn't respond well to someone noticing the things they do well. Encourage a culture where this happens spontaneously and can come from anywhere.

Immediate Action: Tell one person today something they do well: be specific and detailed.

Recognise Life Beyond Work

Everyone you meet will be dealing with some challenges that you almost certainly won't be aware of. When someone isn't performing or delivering, lead with curiosity. Ask open questions and ask what they need to be able to perform. Humans almost invariably respond better to support and encouragement than blame and finger pointing.

Immediate Action: Think of one person in your team who might be struggling. Get in touch and check in on how they are doing. Be 100% present and listen to whatever comes up. Listen and be patient.

Encourage Open Communication

Lead by example with open conversations where your team is able to express their ideas, concerns, and feedback without fear of retaliation. Actively listen to their input and involve them in decision-making processes.

Immediate Action: share with those you work with in an area where you feel uncertain and need help. Ask for ideas. Listen, engage, and acknowledge the help from others to solve the challenges.

Invest in Developing Skills

Provide growth opportunities specific for each person. Training programs, workshops, mentorship, and opportunities for career advancements send a powerful message that you're investing in each person's development.

Immediate Action: Ask one person what they need to help them develop in their role. Be present, listen and make sure you follow up on the conversation.

One of the most important realisations when it comes to putting people first is that people only do things for their reasons. Not your reasons.

And the only way to engage people in your team is to understand what is driving them, to find out what is important to them. Note, it's exactly the same skill we explore in the context of home life.

Ask people open questions. Take the time to listen. Demonstrate you've listened by playing it back to them.

Do what you can to act upon it.

If you can't act upon it, be open about it.

If you're ever stuck, think what any human being would respond to in that situation. Turn the tables. What would you do if you were on the other side of the table?

This takes time and effort to do.

I've yet to meet the ambitious leader who says to me that I've got a spare hour this week and I don't know what to do with it.

It takes that bit of effort to carve out time and space to put people first.

I promise you, it will be worthwhile.

The lazy way is to solely focus on the numbers and results.

The harder way is to focus on building people. Results will follow.

Putting it into practice.

Simple is not the same as easy.

It's simple to say the words "Put People First".

And sometimes so much harder to do in practice. When the pressure is on, quarter end is closing, competitors are shaving your margins and your to-do list is endless.

It takes time and effort to listen and guide and support people.

The truth is that if you want to achieve big bold goals, you simply cannot do it alone. The Big Bold Mindset is all about igniting the passion in the people around you. And that can only happen by finding out what drives each person in your team.

And that requires making a conscious choice and commitment to put more into your people. The research is unequivocal. It's one of the best things you can do to create results. Ditch the old model of the world and work to create time to put people first.

Chapter 10 – Agree on Values

Something wasn't right.

I couldn't put my finger on it, but I had that uneasy feeling in the pit of my stomach.

The "on the surface" conversations all seemed logical and the ideas we talked about made sense.

We were making some small progress but I couldn't shake the feeling that something was awry.

It was an early-stage business where I was the CEO. I had brought a senior team member in who, on paper, had all the right credentials. A wealth of experience and a long list of clients who would follow them.

Very little of that promise was showing up in the business.

I had more than a few broken nights' sleep. My mind working hard to try and figure out what was not working.

On paper it should work. The logic of the plan was compelling.

In reality, it wasn't working.

What had I missed? What could I do differently?

It gnawed away at me.

What experiment could I run, what ideas could I try to do something differently?

The truth will always come out.

I reminded myself of the truth that we only ever do things for our own reasons, not for other people's reasons.

Our reasons are guided by our values. Our values, the things that shape how we think, how we act, how we behave, lead to what shapes our results.

Over lunch I invited a conversation around our values. We took it in turn to share the values that we each held closely.

The insight gave me a eureka experience. In that moment, it became blindingly obvious why things were not progressing. I had made the mistake of overriding emotion with logic.

Sixty percent of our values were absolutely aligned.

Twenty percent of our values were neutral.

Twenty percent of our values were in direct conflict.

We had spent all the time and energy focusing on the area where we were aligned.

It created lots of excitement and buzz.

It was the unspoken conflicting values that were the issue. These were the ones that were hampering progress.

Here's the irritation.

This conversation was always in plain sight and could have been had on day one rather than many months down the track. The truth will always come out. Isn't it far better to find that truth earlier rather than later?

There was also very good news.

Once we had this conversation from a non-judgmental perspective, where we were both open and honest around what was driving us, the solution came very quickly.

We re-structured how we worked together and it removed the blockages to how we work and very quickly led to a sharp rise in the business growth. We had unblocked what was standing in the way of growth.

It doesn't matter if you work with one person or your team is 100,000 strong.

It's exactly the same principle to understand: what values are driving each member of your team, including yourself?

This is the essence of teamwork. This is the essence of we, not me.

Where Are You?

Early in my career, I was cynical about values.

They were described as soft skills.

I had little interest in developing my soft skills. It just felt like a lot of touchy-feely rubbish.

How do you view values?

What is your experience of values in the workplace?

Has it been constructive and helped to shape growth?

Perhaps it's been toxic?

What about you personally? Are you aware of what your personal values are?

Do you have conversations around values? At work or at home?

It's much easier to have conversations around logic and actions we can take to move things forwards.

Much harder, is to have conversations about what is really driving us as individuals.

And yet, this is where the truth of how a team will work together resides. Our values and the conversations we have around these are perhaps the most important conversations we can have in order to work more effectively together as a team.

Let's say for example, for a leader, accountability ranks in your top five values. But, for your project manager, their value lies in creating a 'blame free' culture.

While these are not in opposition directly, your project manager may see 'accountability' as assigning blame, and you'll forever remain in a conflict loop with non-resolution.

Within a team, values shape conversations. And it's our conversations that shape how we act and what our culture becomes. Values are the building blocks of culture.

The Science of Culture

Research findings strongly support the notion that teams with a strong culture, where values align, outperform their peers by a significant margin.

One study[16] covering over 1,000 companies from 42 countries found that those with a strong ethical culture achieved better financial performance and were more likely to attract and retain top talent.

The researchers measured culture using a tool called the Ethical Culture Assessment, which assesses various dimensions of culture, including leadership, approach to climate, and ethical practices.

They then compared the performance of companies with strong cultures to those with weaker cultures.

The study found that companies with strong ethical cultures outperformed their peers in several key metrics. Specifically, companies with strong cultures had:

Better financial performance: Companies with strong cultures had higher financial returns than those with weaker cultures. For every one-point increase in ethical culture scores, companies experienced a 0.9% increase in return on assets.

Higher levels of employee retention: companies with strong ethical cultures were more likely to retain their employees than those with weaker cultures. For every one-point increase in ethical culture scores, companies experienced a 2.7% increase in employee retention.

---

16 Organizational Ethical Culture and Financial Performance: A Meta-Analysis" published in the Journal of Business Ethics in 2021. The study was conducted by researchers Nien-hê Hsieh, Joe J. Broschak, and Zachary Mohr.

These findings are not isolated. Many other studies point towards the positive impact of embracing values and the deliberate shaping of team culture.

You'll be hard pressed to find a leader who doesn't believe that values are important to a team.

And yet, many leaders still don't get it right.

All too often there's a good dose of cynicism inside many teams around culture and values.

Why is this?

Values Done Badly

Have you ever experienced working in a toxic culture?

Perhaps you're in one now? Maybe you know someone who works in such an environment?

An environment where people say one thing and do something else.

An environment where no-one feels safe to speak their truth.

A workplace where you dread turning up to each day.

It gets worse.

Toxic workplace cultures are bad for our health.

One survey of 1,266 employees in a UK public health organisation investigated the relationship between negative workplace culture and employee health outcomes.

Unsurprisingly, those who experienced negative workplace culture were more likely to experience stress, burnout, and depression.

I'd be willing to bet that every workplace like this has a nice sounding set of values somewhere.

On their website, on their walls, in their HR manuals and materials.

So what's gone wrong?

It's not enough to have a set of values.

It's 100% about how those values get implemented throughout the team.

I've yet to meet a business with a set of values that are "Be Unkind", "Do Evil", "Bully Other People".

And organisations that have a culture like this will still have a sweet sounding set of values on the wall. Values that are worthless because no-one believes them.

Big Bold Leaders

Holiday Extras is a successful company that provides parking at airports in the UK.

Recently, I spent time with their senior technical leaders. We explored the areas of values - for them it sits right at the heart of how they have shaped their culture and the growth that followed.

Before I met them, I found their ethos clearly articulated on their website. Not just through words but going deeper into concrete examples of how one lives and displays their values at their very best.

On arriving at their offices outside London, the values are very clearly displayed above the reception area echoing what I'd read on the website.

So far, so good and perhaps not dissimilar to many organisations.

Here's where the difference showed up.

In all the conversations, the team lived their values. They knew what they were. They walked the talk. It was real. Not just nice sounding words.

It showed up in the details: the way the receptionist genuinely thought about what I needed prior to my talk. The questions the team asked showed the importance of personal development being the best version of each other. The way the team interacted, challenged, and supported each other.

And that is the difference. It's about turning those values into real conversations.

This doesn't happen by just displaying them on the website and wall.

It happens by leaders from the top-down living by the same values.

By being consistent.

By making it part of conversations.

By celebrating what people do well when they are acting and living in accordance with the values.

Their values were distinct and unique to them. Not just a set of boiler plate values that any organisation could have.

If you're curious they are:

- Be Courageous
- Be at the Helm
- Be Pioneering in Spirit
- Be One Team
- Be the Best Version of You

They don't just have to be a set of values. They live by a set of values.

That's a big and important difference.

Values to Create Growth

A former colleague from KPMG is now a senior partner at a global financial services firm.

He shared with me a story of how he uses values to create connections outside his firm.

His team was pitching for work with one of the world's largest private equity funds.

The pitch was very simple.

Here are your values.

Here are our values.

Let's explore and talk through why we are a good fit because we are so well aligned in terms of the way we think and the way we behave.

No endless presentations about benefits and what they could be for the client, and how great they were as a firm.

One simple conversation that went to the heart of what matters and unlocked the door.

They won the work and are now one of the firm's largest clients.

Begin at Home

I want to invite you to use a three-step process to think about it in the simplest way possible and run some experiments.

I invite you to this at home. Not at work.

When I first suggested I was going to do values at home, my friends thought I was crazy. They thought I was trying to corporatise my kids.

At the time I wanted to run experiments to find out how we could work better as a family team to successfully and safely sail the world.

It turned out to be one of the best things we have done as a family team. I have positively shaped our conversations and how we are together.

Not just over our two-years round the world, but for all the time before and after how we deal with life's challenges.

Step 1 - Your Values

I'd like to invite you to reflect and write down your values.

What are the values that are most important to you?

If you want some ideas, there is a list at www.CasparCraven.com/values for a list of over 100 commonly held values.

Take some time and reflect on it and write them down.

Step 2 - Team Conversation

Have a conversation with your family or close friends. Ask them what their values are. Explore with curiosity where your values align. Where they are neutral and where they might be different. Are you using different words but actually mean something very similar?

Explore what you do when you live that value at its very best.

See if you can come up with a list of values where you are fully aligned and you all understand what you mean.

When we did this as a family team, it was me, my wife and our three children under the age of 10. We had to simplify the language to make it understandable.

It was that understandable language that I then used at work to have better, more impactful conversations at work.

Step 3 - Living the Values

Without this step, nothing is likely to stick.

This is about working together which says how we fold this into everyday conversations?

At home we created a piece of art to symbolise all our values. It still hangs in our house.

We did exactly the same at work.

At home we created a ritual to talk about what each person had done that day or week to live the values.

We did exactly the same at work.

At home we created small fun prizes to celebrate living the values.

We did exactly the same at work.

By exploring values at home, we transformed how we worked as a home team.

I then took those skills to work and became a better leader at work because of those skills.

At work, I'm certain you will already have a set of values.

It's Step 3 that will be the crucial one. How do you live those values? What can you do as a team to have these better conversations?

If you'd like to go deeper in this important area, you will find more guidance and resources at www.CasparCraven.com/values.

Better Conversations at Work

Getting clear on our values is about understanding what we believe is the most important way to behave. Those values shape what we say and how we interact with others. Those interactions shape our results.

The single best way I know to understand anything is to run it through the filter of the real world. It turns it into a real conversation rather than a corporate jargon conversation.

As humans, we are not thinking creatures that feel. We are feeling creatures that think.

Having the conversations around what's important to each person and bringing those feelings to life and shaping the conversations is a tool that sits at the very heart of the Big Bold Mindset.

Chapter 11 – Unleash Your Superpowers

Why the f**k do they not get it.

I've explained it multiple times and what I'm getting back makes no sense.

It's so frustrating.

Ever had that experience where someone just isn't getting it?

I have.

I'm sure you have.

If it's because someone just isn't interested, then the place to explore is motivation.

If though, someone is trying hard, what's at play? What's going on?

Einstein had something to say on this:

"Everybody is a genius. But if you judge a fish by its ability to climb a tree, it will live its whole life believing that it is stupid."

Achieving a Big Bold Mindset is a team activity.

It's impossible on its own.

The key is recognising that each person has a unique role to play.

And that requires us to unlock the genius in every person.

It's unleashing each person's superpower.

Every single person on this planet has a set of experiences unique to them, a unique set of neurons firing and has something different to offer.

Neurodiversity used to be viewed as a weakness.

It's increasingly viewed as a superpower.

If we start viewing everyone as having a unique perspective on the world, then we can clearly see how they can make a unique contribution.

Centre of the World Thinking

One of the most common traits of the human animal is 'centre of the world' thinking.

The notion that because we think and see things in a certain way, that everyone else does too.

This notion is fundamentally flawed. And yet it's so ingrained.

When someone doesn't understand something, we've explained multiple times, we assume they are wrong because they don't get it.

Instead, we should assume the default position that they see the world differently to us – and that it's a good thing.

Take the notion of strengths.

When we are exceptionally good at doing something, we tend not to value this.

We assume that if we are good at something, then everyone else is as well.

We tend to not be aware of the things we are exceptionally good at. To downplay them.

And conversely, we often give ourselves and others a hard time for the things we are not so good at.

As humans, far too often we have a distorted view of the world. Of ourselves. Of others.

Those who seek to develop a Big Bold Mindset need to harness a wide array of opinions. People who see things differently.

We need these different views so that we can challenge what is true and what is not true.

We need to be able to see what we are facing. The reality of how our team feels, and then shape them accordingly.

Where Are You?

How self-aware are you?

Could you now write down the two or three things you are exceptionally good at doing? Better than just about anyone else you know.

Would these be the same things that other people would say about you?

What about those in your teams at home and at work?

How self-aware are they about what they are exceptionally good at?

Have you ever shared what they are brilliant at with them?

Have you ever had conversations with your team to create a shared understanding of each person's unique brilliance?

The Science of Self-Awareness

Although most people *believe* they are self-aware, research has revealed self-awareness is a truly rare quality.

A team of researchers[17] embarked on a large-scale scientific study of self-awareness covering 10 separate investigations with nearly 5,000 participants.

Their findings were that only 10–15% of the people studied actually fit the criteria of self-awareness.

How was self-awareness defined?

Across the studies, the researchers noticed that two broad categories of self-awareness kept emerging:

Internal vs External Self Awareness

They distinguished two types of self-awareness: Internal self-awareness, how clearly we see and

17 "How Self-Awareness Unlocks Leadership Potential" - https://hbr.org/2018/01/what-self-awareness-really-is-and-how-to-cultivate-it

understand ourselves; and external self-awareness, how much we understand how other people view us.

These two different dimensions were not found to be correlated. The clear advice is doing the work to improve both internal and external self-awareness.

This self-awareness gap is huge.

The benefits of better self-awareness are undisputed. When we see ourselves clearly, we are more confident and creative. We make better decisions, build stronger relationships, and communicate more effectively. We become more effective leaders and are more likely to solve hard challenges.

So why the gap?

Researchers suggest several pitfalls:

Blinded by Confidence

As we become more senior, we are less likely to seek disconfirming evidence or question our assumptions.

The risk of overconfidence also increases. Research suggests that more experienced managers are less accurate in assessing their leadership effectiveness compared with less experienced managers.

In a study of more than 3,600 leaders[18] across a variety of roles and industries it was found that, relative to lower-level leaders, higher-level leaders overvalued their skills (compared with others' perceptions).

---

18 https://hbr.org/2018/01/what-self-awareness-really-is-and-how-to-cultivate-it

This pattern existed for 19 out of the 20 competencies researchers measured, including emotional self-awareness, accurate self-assessment, empathy, trustworthiness, and leadership performance.

Success looks like

In the research they found that the most successful leaders seek frequent critical feedback. They become more self-aware in the process by seeking out feedback from people who have their best interests in mind *and* are willing to tell them the truth.

To ensure they don't overreact or overcorrect based on one person's opinion, they also gut-check difficult or surprising feedback with others.

Stuck in a Rut

Low self-awareness and an unwillingness to take feedback on the chin, are a recipe for repeating mistakes.

Repeating mistakes means progress and growth flat-lines.

One of my favourite formulas comes from Ray Dalio: Pain + Reflection = Progress.

It's sitting with the pain, reflecting on it, seeking to discern the message it's giving you, in order to run the next set of experiments to be able to iterate forwards.

A Big Bold Mindset, by definition, is hard to develop and there are no certainties.

It requires a large number of experiments.

It will be accompanied by many failures.

The failures are guaranteed. The success is not.

It's the willingness to pick over the carcass of another failed experiment that will provide ideas to move forwards.

Absent of the reflective process, being stuck in a rut is certain.

Big Bold Leaders

Marcus Buckingham, in his book *Now, Discover Your Strengths,* makes a powerful case for a strengths-based approach to leadership. By identifying and developing their strengths, individuals and organisations can achieve much greater success than by focusing on their weaknesses.

He argues that too often, people are encouraged to work on improving their weaknesses, which can lead to frustration, burnout, and limited success. His StrengthsFinder assessment, for example, has been used by millions of people around the world to identify their unique talents and strengths.

His approach makes good sense.

By identifying and doubling down on one or two things you are exceptional at, you will get a much higher return on your efforts than by trying to improve a weakness.

The inherent danger of trying to improve on a weakness is running the risk of weakening a strength.

This wisdom has been well accepted by organisations around the world as psychometric tests, such as DISC,

Myers Briggs, and Kolbe, are routinely used to evaluate performance and help with talent development.

Both in my corporate working life and in the leadership development company I run, I have used these tools many times and they absolutely have a place.

I also believe they have two limitations:

They run the risk of being forgotten about as there is typically so much information to digest.

While they may develop a helpful *internal* self-awareness, there is little they provide in terms of raising greater *external* self-awareness.

To overcome these challenges, I would like to share the most impactful strengths-based tool that I have developed. It's a tool our teams routinely use to create better conversations, better team understanding and greater trust in teams around the world. It is also deceptively simple.

Be More Human

People who know you well already know what your superpowers are. All you have to do is ask them.

I still remember when I first did this exercise many years ago. I hand-selected 10 people who I knew well and who I trusted. They were a mix of work colleagues, family, and friends. Some I had known for a long time. Some for only a short time.

The email I sent to them was to ask what they saw as my unique capability, the thing that I naturally do better than most people.

Within a day the responses were in.

I can still remember the words now. Some very kind words that I found very moving.

I printed them all off and with a highlighter, flagged up the golden thread running through all the comments. There were two very distinct themes.

The two themes for me are being able to imagine a bigger picture in the future and bringing together brilliant people to make that picture happen.

I didn't appreciate these characteristics as being unique, I'd always just been like this. But the people who knew me well could see me more objectively than I could.

The feedback was guiding me on the areas I should double down on and where I could create the most growth.

It was serving two purposes that the computer-generated psychometrics couldn't.

It was giving me external self-awareness.

And crucially it was highly memorable because it was in the voices of people I knew and trusted.

Vulnerable Conversations

It was one thing for me to know this. And immensely useful as it was, there was another level.

Our team at work ran the same exercise and we sat round and shared the feedback.

How often do we share with our colleagues the things we are exceptional at? Not very often in my experience.

It can feel awkward for many people to say I'm really good at this.

When we shared the feedback, we'd each realised it was powerful.

It created a sense of vulnerability.

It created trust.

It helped us to better understand who we should approach when we had different challenging situations. We really started to get to know each other better.

Ray Dalio at Bridgewater Associates has a version of this called 'The Baseball Cards'. Each team member has their small handful of strengths on a baseball card. When they get together for meetings, especially with new people they swap cards so they can rapidly understand each other and the expertise in the room.

This is about unleashing the strengths of your team.

The Superpowers Email

Would you like to try this exercise?

There are explainer videos at www.casparcraven.com/super-powers

Want to start right now? Here's the email text to send to between 6 and 10 people to start gathering feedback.

Dear [.............]

I'm on a training programme and I'd really appreciate your help. Would you mind taking a few minutes to help me with a question. What do you see as something that I am

exceptionally good at, my unique capability? Something that I naturally do better than most people?

Would it be possible to get a reply by [...........]

Thank you

Celebrating Differences

The Big Bold Mindset seeks out challenges and hard problems that others haven't yet solved. Doing this with the same level of thinking as most people won't get you far.

It's about teams with diverse ways of thinking, those who are prepared to challenge the norm and people who have different strengths. They are vital.

In your team how much diverse thinking do you have. How many different strengths are you aware of? Do you have someone with remarkable talent who hasn't yet spoken up; but if their strengths were revealed could be a game changer for your goals?

Make it your mission to get to know and understand the strengths and diversity you have in your team. It could be the key to unlocking your growth.

Chapter 12 – Build Your Trust

I sat at the chart table watching the wind instruments.

The wind had consistently blown at 50-55 knots for the last three hours, as we crashed through mountainous seas deep in the Southern Ocean.

The closest land was Antarctica.

It was pitch black outside.

Our eyes constantly scanning the radar checking for icebergs nearby.

In the space of a few minutes, the wind ratcheted. To 60, then 62,63,64,65 knots. Hurricane force winds.

Our sails would be destroyed in anything consistently over 60 knots.

We had no choice but to go on deck to take the sail down.

I called my foredeck team. Guys. We need the sail down now.

This was the ultimate test of trust.

Four men clipped on with thin lifelines had to make their way to the front of the boat to retrieve the sail while our helmsman guided the boat through the huge seas.

Visibility was a few feet in front of you. The wind howling. Battered by the spray from breaking waves.

One slip and it would be certain death over the side in water temperatures just above freezing. The chances of being found in those furious seas, zero.

We had our lives in each other's hands.

The ultimate test of trust. Do I trust you with my life?

A team of people

A team is simply a group of people who trust each other.

I've learnt in the most extreme way possible what it takes to build that trust.

While the consequences in the working world aren't life and death, the principle is exactly the same.

Without trust you have no team. There is no way to achieve that big bold goal.

Will you give all that you've got to make it happen for the team?

Will you put yourself out there for others?

Push yourself beyond your comfort zone.

Without that bedrock of trust, it will not happen.

Ambitious leaders must develop and shape a team who trust each other.

Researchers at MIT Sloan found that teams who trust their leaders are 42 times more likely to be highly resilient.

A team without resilience will not achieve big bold goals. That makes it an absolute prerequisite.

No-one would argue against the need for high levels of trust.

Here's the challenge.

Research from Harvard Business School[19] *shows that 58% of people would trust a stranger before their boss.*

Ouch. Fresh thinking is needed. Decisive action is needed for ambitious leaders to avoid a lack of trust becoming their Achilles heel and sabotaging their big bold goals.

Where Are You?

How self-aware are you of the trust levels in your team?

At work and at home.

Do you trust your team?

Does your team trust you?

I'd wager that if you don't trust your team, they don't trust you either.

When did you last have a conversation about trust?

---

[19] https://universitycollegeblog.du.edu/2021/07/leadership-skills-to-reduce-workplace-drama-and-drive-results/

The Science of Trust

Neuroscientist Paul J Zak in his paper *The Neuroscience of Trust*, sought to explore the neurochemistry behind trust building.

Starting with the question: "Why do two people trust each other?" led him to study several thousand companies and develop a framework based on an understanding of the chemistry happening in our brains.

In what he defined as high-trust organisations, he found teams were more productive, had more energy, and were better at collaborating than people working at low-trust ones.

Zak's research focused on the chemical, oxytocin, a hormone associated with emotional regulation.

They found that when individuals experience trust, oxytocin levels in their brains increase, leading to feelings of warmth, empathy, and connection.

Conversely, when individuals experience distrust, oxytocin levels decrease, leading to feelings of anxiety and suspicion.

Think of trust as a chemical reaction inside each of us.

Viewed in this way, it seems that decoding that chemistry could be helpful. If we understand this, we can choose our actions based on what will trigger that chemical release for building trust.

Although later work has found the chemistry is more complex than a single molecule, the conclusions he found do point to a helpful set of behaviours that were consistently found to increase trust. These included:

Excellence Recognition

The neuroscience shows that recognising a job done well has the largest effect on trust when it occurs immediately after a goal has been met, when it comes from peers, and when it's tangible, unexpected, personal, and public.

Personal Discretion

Being trusted to figure things out is a big motivator. Often, younger or less experienced employees will be the chief innovators, because they're less constrained by what "usually" works. That's how progress was made in self-driving cars.

After five years and a significant investment by the U.S. government in the big three auto manufacturers, no autonomous military vehicles had been produced.

Changing tack, the Defense Advanced Research Projects Agency offered all comers a large financial prize for a self-driving car that could complete a course in the Mojave Desert in less than 10 hours.

Two years later a group of engineering students from Stanford University won the challenge—and $2 million.

Show Vulnerability

Leaders in high-trust workplaces ask for help from colleagues instead of just telling them to do things. The research team found that this stimulates oxytocin production in others, increasing their trust and cooperation. Asking for help is a sign of a secure leader—one who engages everyone to reach goals.

Given our biochemistry will be unique to each person, it seems sensible to conclude that the chemical reactions are different depending on each person. That said, understanding a general structure of what is more likely to build trust is a helpful jumping off point for the "building trust conversations" you will find shortly.

Undermining Trust

Can you recall a leader you worked with who got trust consistently wrong? What were the things they did? Try this as a tick list:

- Their behaviour was inconsistent
- They often ignored or contradicted you
- They put their needs ahead of the team
- They were regularly caught lying
- They were oblivious to the feelings of others
- They didn't believe in transparency
- The never took accountability for their mistakes

You can probably add to the list with things you've experienced.

How many things might you have done in the last month? Either consciously or unconsciously?

It's pretty hard to be perfect and avoid making mistakes. Especially when the pressure is on.

Big Bold Leaders

In 1993 an unknown Taiwanese American entrepreneur cofounded Nvidia, a startup to make computer chips for video games. That company has grown into a juggernaut with annual sales in 2023 of $27 billion dollars.

Jensen Huang, the CEO and cofounder, was voted The World's Best Performing CEO[20] by Harvard Business Review.

Huang is considered by his employees as strong, thoughtful, and authentic - the CEO that anyone would want to work for[21].

The secret sauce is culture.

Specifically, a culture of trust enables teams to collaborate effectively, take risks, and innovate, which has been instrumental in the company's growth and success.

So what exactly do leaders like Huang do?

Open Communication

They've encouraged an environment where individuals feel comfortable expressing their opinions, ideas, and concerns. By fostering a culture of open dialogue, Huang creates a sense of trust and psychological safety, allowing team members to collaborate effectively and share diverse perspectives.

Lead by Example

Leaders set the standard of trustworthiness. By living with integrity, consistency, and ethical behaviour, through actions and decisions, they stick to the value of trust.

---

[20] https://hbr.org/2019/11/the-best-performing-ceos-in-the-world-2019

[21] https://www.thestreet.com/investing/stocks/nvidia-jensen-huang-businessperson-of-the-year-14393724

Empower Others

Teams are given autonomy where individuals are encouraged to take ownership of their projects and make independent decisions. This invites trust as people are more likely to feel valued, respected, and trusted to deliver results.

Explain Decision-Making

Transparency in decision-making processes encourages teams to understand the rationale behind decisions and clear explanations when circumstances require tough choices.

Balance Work and Life

The importance of work-life balance and well-being is prioritised. Acknowledgement of the holistic well-being of teams encourages a healthy work-life integration, and the importance of personal time outside of work.

Huang is a perfect example of the Big Bold Mindset done in a way that puts people first. In his own words:

"We are building one of the world's great technology companies. NVIDIA is a "learning machine" that constantly evolves by seeking challenging opportunities that matter to the world."

And trust is the bedrock of that creating of high-performance that Huang has unquestionably created.

Trust the Conversation

Let's get specific.

What can you do immediately to build greater levels of trust?
Begin it with one conversation.

It could be with one person. It could be with your team.

It could be at work. It could be at home.

You decide where to start.

Perhaps by considering where you feel most comfortable to have the conversation.

Ask the question.

What do we do as a team that builds trust?

What do we do as a team that erodes trust?

What could we do as a team that will build greater levels of trust?

Listen to what comes back and write it down.

Don't try to argue the point if you disagree. Just listen.

When whoever is speaking has finished, ask what else.

When more things come up, write that down too.

Only stop when they have stopped.

Then replay it to make sure you've heard it properly.

Then have a conversation. Are there one or two things that are happening that are eroding trust? Would simply stopping them make a big difference?

Have a conversation around what you could start doing.

Are there things that you currently do that you should continue to do because they are good?

Aim to conclude with a very simple list in simple language of things that you:

Should stop doing.

Should start doing.

Should continue doing.

Complexity kills many ideas and plans. Keep it simple, clear and concise.

The power of this Start/ Stop/ Continue conversation is because we don't experience the world in the same way.

Each of us have been uniquely shaped by our own experience.

If you don't ask your team what builds or erodes trust,

I don't see how it's possible to accurately answer this question with a guess.

Do you imagine that as a team you're more likely to build trust after this conversation?

Trust arrives on foot and leaves on horseback.

Building trust isn't about what you do once in a while.

It's created slowly over time in the micro gestures and behaviours.

At sea in the Southern Ocean, the only reason we could confidently put your life in another person's hands was because of that bedrock of trust that had built over the thousands of ocean miles we sailed together and countless sail changes.

The trust was built day by day.

And yet, one instance would have undermined it all. That's all it would have taken.

One instance where someone wasn't true to their word and the seed of doubt would have been planted.

It's about consistency over time.

This can't be faked.

It has to be genuine.

Humans have a knack for knowing the truth of something.

To be a big bold leader, you need people on the journey with you.

And the only way to do that is by being consistent and showing up as trustworthy.

Make building trust something you think about and focus on. Be deliberate, specific, and conscious.

Give yourself the gift of insight from your team by having the conversation.

And then make darn sure you act on it. Without that trust you have no team.

Theme 4: Bigger by the Day

It's guaranteed on your journey to bigger and bolder things you will get stuck at times.

The best way though to get unstuck, is to not get stuck in the first place!

Forewarned is forearmed.

In the next four chapters, you will find ideas and ways of thinking that others have developed.

Ideas to shape your thinking that will mean you're less likely to get stuck.

Use them to manage your expectations and to develop your Big Bold Mindset so that you can overcome the toughest obstacles.

Let them help you think and act bigger by the day.

Chapter 13 – Inch Yourself Forward

I was feeling overwhelmed.

I didn't know where to start or what to do next.

Projects were half started all over the place and every single one of them had stalled.

I could feel my chest tighten. My blood pressure is rising. My breath quickening.

Uncertain of what to do next.

My mind was spinning. Racing.

Feeling alone and isolated.

The door was kicked wide open for self-doubt to stride into the room.

"What on earth were you thinking? There's no way you can do that project. You must be nuts!"

All I could see was overwhelming challenges.

And zero solutions.

I called a friend.

The challenges poured out of me while she quietly listened.

Just sharing them and getting them out of my head felt better.

I started to gain perspective again and to break the size of the challenge into more manageable pieces. Much smaller pieces against which I could begin to make progress.

Running the risk of only seeing the big picture and not being able to break it into smaller chunks is in truth part of the job description for a leader with a Big Bold Mindset.

Forewarned is forearmed. Cultivating a Big Bold Mindset means knowing that a sense of overwhelm is not only possible but highly likely.

That means, developing a strategy in advance is more than nice to have. It's fundamental.

Inch by Inch

The solution is simpler than you might imagine.

I had actually learnt it many years earlier before drifting to the back of my memory.

I was 10 years old.

I was in a nine-foot dinghy with my dad.

Rowing across a storm-bound bay, we were being swept out to sea in strong winds surrounded by breaking waves.

I was feeling scared.

His words were simple yet impactful.

"Inch by inch is a cinch,

Yard by yard is f******g hard."

That's how we will get back across the way.

One inch at a time.

We'll just be consistent and chip away at it.

He was, of course, right and we got home safely.

It was a lesson in how to think about things when feeling overwhelmed by the size or scale of a project.

Inch by inch.

There's a popular theory that echoes this ethos.

It's called marginal gains theory.

It's about breaking down any task or project into much smaller elements against which progress can be made one day at a time.

Where Are You?

When was the last time you achieved a goal that once seemed impossible?

How did you achieve it?

Did it all happen in one day?

Or was it broken down into hundreds, if not thousands of much smaller mini steps?

The answer of course is obvious.

It's the mini steps, the inch-by-inch process.

Reflect on what worked best for you and your strategies to achieve previous goals. What did you learn from those processes? What did you learn that you could use again?

The Math of Marginal Gains

Albert Einstein described compounding as the eighth wonder of the world.

The maths behind marginal gains theory can be understood through the concept of compounding.

Marginal gains theory is about small, incremental improvements in different areas that accumulate and compound over time to produce significant overall gains.

For example, imagine that each marginal gain returns 1% improvement every day.

Over the course of one year, that equates to 1.01 to the power of 365, this equates to 37.78 x improvement.

That means that if you make a 1% improvement every day for a year, the cumulative effect of these daily gains would be equivalent to approximately 3778% better off than where you started.

The consistency of small improvements every single day is what leads to significant overall growth.

The theory became popularised by the strategies used by the British cycling team.

Instead of relying on major breakthroughs or dramatic changes, they looked to identify and implement small adjustments in areas such as equipment, training methods, nutrition, and team dynamics.

It was an approach allowing them to enhance performance and gain a competitive edge.

An approach that led them to dominate the cycling world where, in the Beijing 2008 Olympics, the British Cycling team won 60% of the gold medals they competed for.

The core underlying element is consistent improvement.

Failing to Reach the South Pole

Inconsistency can be fatal.

In 1912, explorer Robert Scott led one of two teams competing to be the first people to reach the South Pole.

Scott's team pressed hard when the weather allowed and hunkered down when the weather was harsh. It made for inconsistent progress and a burnt-out team who sadly perished.

It was in contrast with the Norwegian team who made a 20 mile march every single day come rain or shine. They made it to the Pole and survived.

A lack of inconsistency in your projects might not kill you, but it could kill the project.

How many stalled projects can you think of where the ball has been dropped because of inconsistency?

Big Bold Leaders

Julia Hartz is the co-founder and CEO of Eventbrite. In 2006, she and her fellow co-founders imagined an easily accessible self-service platform to sell tickets for events.

One of the principles driving their success was their application of the concept of marginal gains.

This inch-by-inch process was applied to refine the user experience. By making a large amount of small incremental changes, they could optimise how a user created an event, how the checkout process worked and enhanced the overall navigation of the platform.

This enabled them to consistently create and improve an efficient, user-friendly experience for both event organisers and attendees.

Marginal gains thinking was applied to improving their event discovery and recommendations engine. By continually making small adjustments to their algorithms and studying user behaviour patterns, they fine-tuned the platform's recommendations to better match users' interests and preferences.

These marginal gains in event discovery help drive engagement and increase ticket sales.

Marginal gains were applied to optimisation of their mobile application. Through consistent iterative experiments and improvements, Eventbrite has created a smooth mobile experience for event organisers and attendees, enabling them to manage and access their events on the go.

Marginal gains were applied to the process of consistently gathering customer feedback to understand their pain points and gather insights. By carefully considering and implementing customer feedback, they have made iterative changes to address user needs, leading to improved customer satisfaction and loyalty.

It's been an effective strategy for the Hartz team. Eventbrite are market leaders in their sector and are valued at $700m. A Big Bold idea backed by consistent implementation.

Change Happens in the Calendar

I have two simple ideas for you to consider and experiment with. Both are built on the idea that it's the consistent daily progress that you make that will add up to significant change over time.

Rigorous Attention to Detail

As the saying goes, the devil is in the detail.

Some people love being in the detail. Some, like me, don't especially enjoy it.

Whether it's your sweet spot or not, there is no question you will need this skill set on your team.

In my family team, it's my wife who is all over the detail. We have a standing joke that if it was down to her, it would never get started and if it was down to me, it would never get finished.

Knowing that is good because it means you bring people into your team who are strong where you are weak.

The process for paying attention to the details and making those continuous steps every day is this:

Step 1 - Identify - consider all the possible areas where you can make improvements.

Step 2 - Analyse - study each component and identify potential areas for marginal gains. Look for small changes, adjustments, or optimisations that can be made to enhance performance or productivity.

Step 3 - Prioritise - which areas will have the biggest impact. Focus on these first.

Step 4 - Micro Goals - define specific goals for each component which will help provide a clear direction, enabling you to track progress.

Step 5 - Go - Start implementing the changes and improvements in each area. This could involve experimenting with new strategies, adopting new tools or technologies, refining processes, or acquiring new knowledge or skills. Remember, the key is to focus on small, incremental changes rather than drastic overhauls.

Step 6 - Measure - regularly monitor and track the progress you're making in each area. Keep records of your improvements and assess how they are contributing to your overall goals. This allows you to identify what is working and what needs further adjustment.

Step 7 - Evolve - Continuously iterate and improve: Reflect on your progress, learn from the outcomes, and iterate on your approach. Look for additional opportunities for marginal gains and keep refining your strategies. Focus on constant improvement and adaptability.

Step 8 - Listen - seek feedback and learn from others: Actively seek feedback from others, such as mentors, colleagues, or experts in the field. They can provide valuable insights, suggestions, or perspectives that you might not have considered. Learn from their experiences and incorporate relevant advice into your own practice.

Above all, stay consistent and committed.

The notion of Inch by Inch requires consistent effort and commitment over time. Stay disciplined and maintain your focus on continuous improvement. Small changes can add up to significant progress when practised consistently.

The Single Most Important Thing Today

Each morning, I suggest you consider what is the single most important thing you need to achieve that day.

To take time to reflect on all the to-do list items and write down that one thing.

I prefer using a paper diary to map my time day by day. The type of A5 diary that has one page per day.

At the top of the page I write that one thing down.

Of course there are many other things, but the clarity on the single most important thing means it is more likely to be achieved and to contribute to that incremental, relentless progress.

As an ambitious leader, you will have many demands on your time, energy, and focus. Having a process ensuring you have achieved your single most important task of the day means that you are building in continuous progress and growth towards your goals.

It's Not a Sprint

The Big Bold Mindset knows that overnight success is not a thing.

This is about the marathon and not the sprint.

It's about the continuous set of experiments, of the repetitions needed to make big things happen.

Inch by Inch. Day by Day.

Develop the process to break each project down into its key elements and find the ways to develop all those small improvements which over time will compound.

On the BT Global Challenge, no stone was left unturned for us to find the 1% improvements in every area we could imagine.

The tiny 2-millimetre continuous adjustments to how we set the sails for each wind angle we sailed.

Interrogating every single item on the boat to work out if we really needed it in order to reduce weight so we could improve boat speed. Right down to the level of cutting off the handle of each person's toothbrush.

Continuously monitoring the performance of each helmsman in different wind and sea conditions so that we could work out who would steer in different conditions.

The focus was relentless. The attention to detail was on every small thing.

When we beat another boat by 10 seconds after racing for over 40 days, it's easy to see just how much impact each micro experiment and improvement can make.

Sometimes, that can be all the difference between first place and last place.

Finding the right person with the skills to lead the marginal gains work on your Big Bold Goals to make this happen is essential.

The Big Bold Mindset knows that when you are consistent, compounding will do its magic.

Chapter 14 – Harness Your Habits

He was lurking just behind one of the plants by the office doors.

I could understand why.

For the past week I had arrived late to the office and it was getting later every day…0905, 0910, 0915.

My boss had had enough and wanted to catch me coming in late to give me a piece of his mind.

In truth, I deserved it.

I wasn't looking after myself and I certainly was not doing good work.

I was drinking most evenings.

I was smoking.

Zero exercise.

Overweight.

Eating at Burger King more times a week than was healthy.

A junk food diet at home.

Staying up late.

Getting up late to catch the rush-hour tube, feeling sluggish and lethargic.

No big bold goals were on the horizon.

No big bold goals would have been possible.

This was my working life in the City in my early twenties.

Roll forward three decades and the world seems very different.

There is much greater recognition of the importance of looking after ourselves, of putting us in the best shape possible to achieve whatever is important to us.

What's Changed

There is a very rapidly growing body of research focused on longevity and health.

We now know more about how we can live healthier, longer lives.

David Sinclair is a Professor of Genetics at Harvard Medical School. In his thought-provoking book *LifeSpan*, he paints a picture of average life expectancy to increase to 120 within the next decade.

He is one of a number of scientists working to chart a course for us all to live more vital and active lives.

Just a decade ago, the received wisdom for healthy living consisted largely of food and exercise suggestions.

The body of work evolving now, points to a much more nuanced, personalised, and far-reaching approach to increasing longevity.

Healthy living is essential for the Big Bold Mindset.

The Big Bold Mindset seeks out challenges and opportunities that demand consistently high levels of energy over long periods of time.

Healthy habits, those daily rituals that are associated with a longevity mindset are joined at the hip with the Big Bold Mindset.

The longevity mindset seeks out fresh ideas to health and human performance for today and to be able to function in peak condition far into the future.

Where Are You?

When did you last undertake a root and branch review of how you live?

A view that puts each of your habits and rituals under the microscope.

When did you last study what is best for you?

In truth, this is a very fast-moving field and it's about keeping informed and becoming very clear about what works for you.

It's about finding the right set of routines and habits.

Take a moment now to reflect and think:

What is something you do that puts you in the *best* place possible to achieve your goals?

What is something you do that puts you in the *worst* place possible to achieve your goals?

What is one thing that you can do more of?

What is one thing that you can do less of?

Make a note and action it.

The Science of Habit

There are many scientists who have views on healthy habits. Habits that are beneficial for developing a Big Bold Mindset.

To spark thinking as to some avenues for you to explore, I've included a tiny selection of some recent findings across a number of subjects.

Mental Health

Dr Gabor Maté has extensively explored the connection between poor mental health and its impact on shortening life span.

For example, Maté emphasises that high stress levels, which are often rooted in adverse childhood experiences and trauma, can lead to long-term physiological changes in the body.

Prolonged exposure to stress hormones like cortisol can disrupt immune function, increase inflammation, and contribute to the development of various physical health conditions, including cardiovascular diseases, diabetes, and autoimmune disorders.

Relationships

Robert Waldinger is a psychiatrist and the director of the Harvard Study of Adult Development, one of the longest-running studies on human happiness and well-being.

Waldinger's research highlights that the quality of our relationships plays a crucial role in our overall well-being and longevity.

The study, which began in 1938 and continues to this day, has followed two groups of participants: one composed of Harvard College graduates and the other of disadvantaged inner-city men.

The study has examined various aspects of their lives, including physical health, mental well-being, relationships, and satisfaction.

Key findings from Waldinger's research indicate that close, supportive relationships significantly contribute to a longer and happier life.

Good-quality relationships, characterised by trust, emotional intimacy, and mutual support, have been linked to better physical health, improved cognitive function, and a higher overall sense of well-being.

Social isolation and loneliness have been associated with poorer health outcomes and a decreased life span.

Rest

Dr Saundra Dalton-Smith is known for her work on rest and its importance for overall well-being. In her research, she has found that rest goes beyond simply sleep and relaxation.

She introduces seven types of rest: physical, mental, emotional, social, sensory, creative, and spiritual. Each type plays a vital role in restoring and rejuvenating our bodies and minds.

Sleep

Professor Matthew Walker is his book *Why We Sleep* explores the critical role that sleep plays in our overall health and well-being.

Sleep is not just a period of rest but a fundamental biological process necessary for our physical, mental, and emotional functioning.

Sleep deprivation is linked to a wide range of health problems, including increased risks of obesity, diabetes, cardiovascular diseases, and mental health disorders such as depression and anxiety. It also impairs cognitive function, memory consolidation, learning abilities, creativity, and decision-making skills.

The Impact of Inaction

The world has changed. Have you?

Have you changed how you lead yourself and your daily habits?

In a competitive world where leaders are pushing the boundaries, those with the most vitality will be the ones best placed to capitalise on opportunities.

In my old world, there was nothing vital. Nothing energised. It was sluggish and as far removed from a Big Bold Mindset as you can imagine.

Imagine friends and peers living a healthy life to the age of 120 and beyond?

Wouldn't you want to put yourself in the best place possible to be there and to continue to do your most important work to make a positive impact on the world. Accept the traditional mindset or embrace the changes in the world brought about by our rapidly accelerating science and knowledge behind what it takes to live a vital life.

The choice is yours.

Optimised Leadership

Many CEO groups I am part of regularly invite leading experts to share their ideas around best habits to optimise health. It's an area that leaders are paying significantly increased attention to.

The truth though, is that few of us have enough time in the day to review the latest science and form our own opinions.

I like to use a sifting mechanism to find the best ideas.

Follow the insights of people who have a fascination within this area, those who regularly interview and dissect the latest findings.

Groundbreaking scientists usually find their way to most, if not all of these media outlets.

Some names to consider following if you are not already doing so are:

Rich Roll, Tom Bilyeu, Dr Ranjan Chatterjee, Andrew Huberman. There are many others!

The Habits Chart

I have a deceptively simple yet powerful tool to share with you. It's a tool that I use every single day to lead myself.

By following this, it puts me in the best place possible to achieve my goals.

It's a one pager I have created called my Habits Chart.

Listed across the top of the sheet are the days of the week.

Listed down the left-hand side are the specific habits I want to hold myself accountable to.

It started with one habit.

Pick one habit that perhaps you are already leaning towards or do some of the time.

Print off this sheet and put it somewhere visible where you will see it every day (remembering the Kahneman principle of what you see is all there is)

Then each day tick off when you have done that habit.

At the end of each week score yourself and how well you did.

I record these on a different sheet which has 1 through 52 on each line for each week of the year.

It's a simple yet powerful way of nudging yourself to remember to do things which you have decided are right for you.

Science shows that on average it takes 66 days[22] to ingrain/ develop a new habit.

I have found it beneficial to think about adding one new habit every 90 days, so four new habits a year.

It's a case of walking rather than running.

Imagine a year from now, what the impact of four newly ingrained helpful habits would be for you?

Diet. Exercise. Writing. Dedicating time to relationships. Anything you can imagine.

I've yet to meet an ambitious person sitting around with lots of time on their hands.

This is about setting the autopilot going on how you lead and manage yourself.

This is about applying marginal gains to how you lead your life.

Will there be weeks when you have a rubbish score and barely do anything on your list?

Almost certainly!

Don't sweat it. This is the system of nudges to get you back on track.

Experiment with Everything

Look for ideas which resonate with you and consider what experiments you can run with.

---

[22] https://www.ucl.ac.uk/news/2009/aug/how-long-does-it-take-form-habit

Try the suggested approach for a month and see your results.
Does it work for you? Do it some more.

If it doesn't work, move onto the next experiment.

For example, over the last year, some experiments that I have tried that I have found that work for me and that have been added to my habits chart are:

Hydrating. Starting the day with a pint of lemon water and a pint of celery juice.

Intermittent fasting. I use what is called a 16:8 plan so I only eat in an 8-hour window and fast for 16 hours a day.

Mental Health. I see a Kinesiology Therapist monthly to keep me on track with my mental health.

Alcohol. I have found for me that a no or very low alcohol lifestyle suits me best and enables me to perform at my optimum.

Future experiments I have planned are around understanding my gut health and personalising my diet around this.

Experiments that I started five years ago and continue to use are around daily cold showers, mediation, careful sleep management and regular exercise.

These are highly personal. I'm not suggesting you follow my habits.

I'm suggesting you form your own hypothesis and use the habits chart as you construct and run your own experiments to find out what works for you.

If you'd like to get my latest habits chart, connect with me on LinkedIn and I can share it with you.

How Long Do You Want to Live?

The notion of longevity is an example of a Big Bold Mindset.

People like David Sinclair who are challenging traditional thinking around how long we live.

His notion is that ageing itself is a disease.

And that this is what we should be treating rather than symptoms of ageing.

This is a big bold concept. A different way of thinking about how we live our lives.

I invite you to challenge yourself on your concepts of health and vitality.

Learn, reflect, and run experiments to find what is right for you. This is an exciting time to be alive.

We have an opportunity to redefine what our lives look like! Imagine going from an expectation of living to 80 and then adding an extra 50% and living to 120 in vibrant health!

Chapter 15 – Invest in Learning

Tracey's school was rated as failing.

The British schools' regulator, Ofsted, was breathing down its neck with inspectors peering into their day-to-day activities.

The performance targets were relentless.

Beyond the results, the pressures were everywhere.

Tight budgets.

Rising costs.

Demotivated staff.

Challenging kids.

Mental-health issues.

Concerns over online bullying.

Demanding parents.

It's a picture across many schools in the UK.

Over the years, I've spoken at plenty of Head Teacher and School Conferences to get insights into the challenging world of education.

Tracey's story as a head teacher at an inner-city school in London stands out.

She wanted and needed to raise the bar.

Tracey realised in order to best serve her students she needed to help them reach higher standards. She needed to approach things with a fresh mindset.

It wasn't that the kids weren't smart, they were. In fact, they were the most resourceful group of young people she'd ever met.

It wasn't that they didn't have the motivation to learn, she could see that in their eyes, as they showed up despite the challenges they faced at home.

It wasn't that…

She recognised the kids didn't know *how* to learn.

They didn't know that their first attempt at a new subject was not a sign of ability, but a step in the right direction.

They didn't know they had permission to get it wrong until they got it right.

They didn't know that failing is part of the learning process.

They didn't know that they could learn as a group, where everyone helped each other.

These kids were so used to doing it on their own, they didn't realise they could rely on their peers for help.

How could Tracey break the cycle?

She decided that she and her fellow teachers needed to role model how to think about the learning process.

That process of struggling, failing, of looking for different ways to approach things, of keeping on going until a breakthrough finally came.

But how to do that?

How could they teach their kids these skills?

She landed on an idea that both the students and the teachers would seek out something new to learn.

Something where no-one had any prior expertise.

Where it was a level playing field.

Where the teachers were absolute beginners too.

They landed on Circus Skills.

So, the school brought in a trainer who taught them skills together.

Through this lens, the kids could see the growth mindset modelled firsthand by the teachers.

They could see the process of struggle.

Of not giving up.

Of asking for help and advice.

Of not being embarrassed by failing on the way to learning.

At the conference where Tracey shared the story, she also shared the hugely positive impact on their results transforming the school results.

They went from failing tests to outstanding records.

She had found an effective way to teach the children how to learn.

Learning how to learn is the lifelong skill that can be the key to unlocking the challenges on the path to achieving big bold goals.

The Growth Mindset

I used to think that human qualities were carved in stone – you were smart or you weren't, and failure meant that you weren't.

It was a narrative I held for too many years.

The result of which was playing small.

Never leaving my comfort zone for fear of failure.

Science has comprehensively debunked the myth of human qualities being set in stone.

Psychologist Carol Dweck has led the way.

Dweck's core finding from 30 plus years of research is that the view you adopt for yourself profoundly affects the way you lead your life.

This view shapes the person you become and what you achieve.

She creates a simple distinction between what she calls a 'fixed mindset' and a 'growth mindset'.

In a fixed mindset, we believe we have a fixed set of abilities, a predetermined range of talents and capabilities and we are either naturally good at something or we are not.

Every situation you face is a test of your intelligence, personality, and character.

In this view of the world, every situation is evaluated, and it feels like you will either succeed or fail, you will look smart or dumb, you will be accepted or rejected.

It is very binary.

It's an exhausting place to be.

With a fixed mindset, you seek to avoid failure and you want to put on display the very best side of you.

To be opened up to failure and criticism feels vulnerable and you seek ways to avoid that feeling.

You seek out certainty and stick only to what you know.

It's easy to see how the seeds for a fixed mindset can be sown early on in life.

Growing up, a child who is praised for being bright, talented or gifted becomes certain that they have a set of God-given skills and talents.

There is no effort required in their performance, they are just naturally gifted, and their success is just about proving how smart or talented they are.

Dweck shares the story of Mrs Wilson, her sixth-grade teacher:

"We were seated around the room in IQ order and only the highest IQ students could be trusted to carry the flag or take a note to the principal.

"She was creating a mindset in which everyone in the class had one consuming goal – look smart, don't look dumb.

"Who cared about or enjoyed learning, when our whole being was at stake every time she gave us a test or called on us in class?"

The growth mindset is the polar opposite.

Growth mindset is the belief that we are all capable of learning and developing new skills.

A growth mindset embraces challenges, sees failures as opportunities for growth, and values the process of learning and improvement.

With a growth mindset, individuals believe that their talents and abilities can be cultivated over time and that they have the potential to improve in any given area.

With a growth mindset, setbacks and obstacles are seen as temporary hurdles that can be overcome with perseverance and the right strategies.

It's a mindset that encourages individuals to take risks, step out of their comfort zones, and continuously seek new opportunities for growth.

People with a growth mindset have a thirst for knowledge and actively seek out opportunities to learn and expand their understanding.

A growth mindset fosters resilience and adaptability in the face of adversity. Individuals are better equipped to bounce back from setbacks, adjust their strategies, and find alternative paths towards their goals.

Dweck's research points conclusively to the fact that people have more capacity for lifelong learning and brain development than they ever thought possible.

People with a growth mindset know that an individual's true potential is unknown and unknowable; that it is impossible to foresee what can be accomplished with years of passion, toil, and training.

With this mindset comes the belief that the qualities and skills a person would like can be developed through a passion for learning.

Where Are You?

Where do you sit?

Growth mindset or fixed mindset?

If it was rated a scale of 1 to 100, where would you rate yourself in terms of a growth mindset?

Where 1 is the view that your talents and abilities are given to you at birth, the die is cast, and you just accept your lot. And where 100 is no limit to what you can learn and achieve. You are relentlessly curious and a lifelong learner.

Where would you score yourself?

Do you tend to seek out information that proves what you currently believe to be true?

Or do you tend to seek out information with the potential to prove you wrong?

Is there an area or field where you are an expert in that field?

Do you know all there is to know?

Or do you find that the more you know the more you realise you don't know.

The good news is that this number is a choice.

You can cultivate a growth mindset.

You can become more curious.

You can increase your learning rate.

The Science of Adaptability

The scientific underpinning for Dweck's works is neuroplasticity.

Neuroplasticity is the term used to refer to the brain's ability to change and adapt throughout our lives.

It's what allows our brain to reorganise its structure, function, and connections in response to our experiences.

The term itself comprises two words: 'neuro' refers to the neurons or nerve cells that are the basic building blocks of the brain, and 'plasticity' refers to the brain's malleability or ability to be shaped and modified.

It's this plasticity that enables the brain to adapt to changing circumstances and the acquiring of knowledge.

It is where the brain reorganises itself to form new neural connections and pathways.

One study[23] explored the effects of intensive language learning on brain plasticity. Adults who learned a new language over a short period of time showed significant changes in brain connectivity and increased grey matter volume.

Another study [24] investigated the effects of music training on neuroplasticity in older adults. It revealed that older adults who engaged in music training showed improvements in auditory processing, attention, and memory, along with changes in brain structure and connectivity.

The punchline is that with practice and effort, new skills and knowledge can be acquired.

Our ability to continuously grow and learn is something that we should never stop cultivating.

Big Bold Leaders

“Before I begin telling you what I think, I want to establish that I'm a dumb shit who doesn't know much relative to what I need to know.

Whatever success I've had in life has had more to do with my knowing how to deal with my not knowing than with anything I know.”

These are the opening words in the book *Principles* by Ray Dalio.

---

[23] https://www.ncbi.nlm.nih.gov/pmc/articles/PMC6529595/ - Nature Communications 2020

[24] https://www.frontiersin.org/articles/10.3389/fnins.2021.630829/full

Principles is a masterclass in applying a growth mindset.

Dalio is the billionaire founder of Bridgewater Associates, the world's largest hedge fund.

It didn't start out that way.

In 1982, fuelled by hubris, Dalio made some poor decisions and Bridgewater was on the point of failure.

At his lowest point, Dalio had to borrow $4,000 from his parents to be able to pay his rent.

This began his journey of humility, an essential quality of a growth mindset.

The questioning process in his mind changed.
It went from "I'm right" to "how do I know I'm right?".

Instead of seeking evidence to prove he was right.

He sought out evidence to challenge his views.

Thoughtfully disagreeing, seeking out different perspectives is critical to developing our thinking and our skills.

For making better decisions for ourselves.

Dalio went further.

He considered how to do this at scale for his team.

At Bridgewater, they built systems and processes to scale the concepts of a growth mindset.

An environment of an idea meritocracy where the best ideas won out rather than the ideas from the highest paid person.

An environment where people are continually getting feedback on how they can improve.

A system called the Dot Collector gets used in meetings that allows people to express their thoughts and see others' thoughts in real time, and then helps them collectively reach an idea-meritocratic decision.

Processes where each decision is viewed as an experiment. Where the assumptions behind each decision are written down in advance and reviewed and reflected on after the experiment.

It is an environment of continuous learning.

It is all about learning to make better decisions.

Stuck in a Loop

Do you recall having been stuck in a recurring loop?

Perhaps you are in one now?

A place where you keep making the same mistakes over and over again?

Where you think you are changing things but in reality, nothing is changing.

Feedback loops and the willingness to embrace them are the name of the game.

Without feedback loops, we have no idea what experiments we need to run next.

We run the risk of spinning our wheels. Of not being able to make progress.

Without a willingness to embrace the feedback, there won't be change.

The fixed mindset says these are my talents, my skills and that is that.

This mindset is destined to stay stuck.

The price of refusing to embrace learning is an acceptance to stay where you are and not progress.

My hunch is that since you're here reading this, you're not willing to settle.

Let's get practical.

Sharpen your Learning Muscle

Learning how to learn again is simple. Simple of course is not the same as easy!

I have a challenge for you.

A challenge and a set of instructions.

Remember the circus skills example?

I invite you to think of a skill, an activity where you have zero expertise. Something which you have a potential interest in. It could be a sport: rowing, tennis, snowboarding. It could be a language. It could be a skill, knitting, creative writing, or pottery.

It could be anything where there is a new set of skills.

Choose your new subject and find an instructor. Then commit to the learning process. Keep a notebook to track your progress and where you struggle.

Take a beginner's mindset. Accept that you are starting from zero and will make many mistakes.

Get comfortable with being uncomfortable. Embrace the mistakes. Don't be afraid to fail. Watch how you react.

Do you lean into failure with curiosity to press on? Or do you lean away and take the failure as a body blow and start seeking out reasons to give up.

How you do anything is how you do everything.

This challenge is designed to sharpen your learning muscle.

Perhaps if you've not been in a classroom and failed at anything for a long time, this may be uncomfortable.

Good.

It means you're doing something beyond your comfort zone and exposing yourself to learning and growth.

The Big Bold Mindset, by its nature, is seeking growth.

One Stroke at a Time

Two years ago, my two eldest children were learning to row at school.

It was a sport that had interested me in the past but it was something I had never done.

I was drawn to the fact that my kids were more expert than I was and I could model the beginner's mindset, the learning mindset to them.

To not be afraid of failure.
Of making an idiot of myself.

At the age of 49, I joined my local rowing club and stepped into an eight-man rowing boat for the first time.

Over the past two years I have been training three times a week.

I've been in a boat where the rest of the crew are much more experienced than me and I am the novice.

I've exposed myself to failure.

I've consistently been getting feedback on how to improve.

Especially when I capsized our four-man boat and we all went swimming with a full crowd of people watching.

Take the lessons and keep moving.

What did it teach me?

Honestly. It made me realise my sharpness to learning and adapting was not as highly attuned as I thought it was.

It exposed that I was actually a slower learner, not the fast learner I had in my internal story.

That sharpened me up.

That's a mindset I now take to all other areas of my working life.

It showed me I need to work harder to learn.

To not be complacent. To keep striving. To stay hungry.

See what your experiments will reveal about your learning style.

To sharpen your approach to learning will sharpen your Big Bold Mindset.

It's not just you.

What about your team?

At home or work?

What could you do as a team to increase your learning skills?

What fun could you have sharpening your skills together?

It doesn't matter who is right. It only matters what is right.

To turn my struggling business around, I had to let go of my ego.

Beforehand I had to be right.

Being right validated who I was.

I made a choice that I would prefer to value myself for being a learner rather than being right.

As a family team we created a large painting which is on our kitchen wall.

It says ***We Are Learners.***

Our kids created the pictures to illustrate all the different ways that we learn.

In my business we adopted a mantra which I still use to this day:

It doesn't matter who is right. It only matters what is right.

Chapter 16 – Push Past Perfect

It was brutal.

We had taken way too long.

Our competition was not taking prisoners.

Long standing clients were having their heads turned as they switched from our product to the competitor's.

In new pitches we were coming in second place.

We were losing and we knew it.

The worst part was that it was all avoidable.

Two years earlier, we had innovated and created a market-leading product.

We were setting the standard.

Charging premium prices.

The de facto brand winning household name clients.

All the signals necessary to attract competitors to what we were doing!

Competition started slowly at first.

Our head start gave us an unfounded confidence that we would stay ahead.

That groundless confidence showed up as perfectionism.

We knew our product had to evolve.

We knew we needed to take customer feedback and keep adapting.

The challenge was we were too slow moving.

We were waiting for 'perfect'.

At each juncture of the product development, we agonised over small details.

Endless internal debates.

Back and forth. Back and forth.

Our loyal customers were forthcoming with helpful feedback. They knew what would help them.

We were just too slow.

Our competitors accelerated faster.

Shipped new updates more quickly.

Ran experiments and iterations faster.

Customers switched as their product had become better faster.

Lightly Held to Tightly Held

It's a tricky line to walk.

The line of perfect.

How tightly one holds onto the concept of perfect.

Should you hold it lightly or tightly?

Lightly holding onto perfect with too little attention to detail invites shoddy careless work.

Tightly holding on with too much perfectionism risks missing the opportunity, as we did.

It's about striking that right balance of attention to detail and to being able make progress.

Our experiments around Past Present Future highlight we don't all look at the world the same way. We all have our own distinct biases.

In exactly the same way, we will all have our own biases in relation to perfectionism.

Some are paralysed by it.

Some are so far from it that it lacks credibility!

The big idea here is that of course we should strive towards perfect and at the same time not to be held hostage by it so that it stops us making progress.

It's knowing when to tightly hold to perfect, and when to lightly hold to perfect.

Where Are You?

What is your natural default setting for making progress?

If you were to imagine our scale of 1-100.

Where 1 is slap dash and just go with minimal preparation,

And 100 is obsessing endlessly about every single detail.

Where would you land?

What is your number?

What about those in your team - at work and at home?

The mindset to achieve big bold goals knows that we need diversity of thinking.

The truth is we need both the attention to detail and the drive to keep moving forward. It's the tension between those two different perspectives that is important.

The struggle to be the very best version possible with the tools and resources that you have and to get things moving.

The Science of Perfectionism

What is perfect anyway?

The Oxford English Dictionary defines perfection as the condition, state, or quality of being free from defect, flawlessness, faultlessness.

Looking to the future, a world where disruption and change is everywhere, the notion of being flawless or free from defect is itself a flawed concept.

I'd suggest there is no such thing.

Only ever a perpetual state of change, of evolution, as we adapt to a changing world.

The now common use of the word 'iteration' should tell us everything we need to know about the pursuit of perfection. It is a process.

The truth is though that perfectionism does exist.

Looking to the past, The Harvard Business Review[25] combed through four decades of research, some 95 different studies covering 25,000 people on perfectionism.

Some findings stood out:

Perfectionism and Performance are not related to each other.

Perfectionists are not better or worse performers than non-perfectionists.

Perfectionism is unlikely to be constructive at work. In fact, it appears to be the opposite. That the trait of perfectionism is more likely to lead to burnout and a negative impact on wellbeing.

It would seem that commonly received wisdom of perfect being a good thing is not actually a good thing.

---

[25] https://hbr.org/2018/12/the-pros-and-cons-of-perfectionism-according-to-research

And yet this notion persists in many workplaces as being an admirable thing to aim at.

Dr Thomas Curran at the London School of Economics has researched what he calls the dark side of perfectionism.[26]

"While many people view perfectionism as a 'necessary evil' that helps people become highly successful, it is a myth.

"There is a lot of evidence to say you are not going to get any real performance benefit from perfectionism, and that it's actually really damaging for lots of people."

His findings connect the rise of perfectionism to the growing number of cases of mental illnesses – such as eating disorders, anxiety, and depression – particularly among young people.

The constant presence of social media in people's lives since the late 2000s has also accelerated this trend: "Images of others at carefully selected moments of their lives have distorted our perceptions of their lifestyles and careers.

It's an increasing trend but it doesn't have to be this way.

One solution Dr Curran suggests is to focus on the process of what we are doing rather than just the end goal.

To focus on learning and growth.

---

26 https://www.lse.ac.uk/research/research-for-the-world/health/over-stressed-and-under-pressure-the-problem-with-being-perfect

It's a finding that aligns with Dweck's advice to focus on a growth mindset which by definition is all about curiosity and learning.

Dr Curran goes further and is an advocate of perfectionism being listed within the Diagnostic and Statistical Manual of Mental Disorders, which is used globally by mental-health professionals in diagnosing issues. Perfectionism has a unique set of symptoms and causes those who experience it harm.

Being perfect at something sounds innocuous, desirable and seeps into our everyday language as we strive for more.

Within that innocuous language there is a darker side, a less helpful side that is seldom held up to the light of day.

An obsession with details that loses sight of what is commercially important to move a project forward.

An obsession with details that aren't actually aligned with the overall mission.

It is a concept that seems desirable but actually needs to be held in check.

The research points to the fact that perfectionism is fool's gold.

Missing the Boat

What have you missed out on by waiting for perfection?

One couple we knew missed out on achieving their life's dream.

They had planned their adventure for years.

Obsessed over the small details.

Worked incredibly hard to get themselves in a place where they could sail the world.

Their boat was in Southampton on the South Coast of England at the same time that we were due to set sail.

That was seven years ago.

Their boat is still there and they will never leave.

Why?

Because they are waiting for perfection.

They are waiting to have their to-do list completed.

They have missed the boat.

Literally and metaphorically.

And until they change how they view perfection; they will always miss the boat?

It has cost them their dream.

What has waiting for perfection cost you?

Big Bold Leaders

Sara Blakely is a leader who personifies taking imperfect action and being willing to learn and improve through experience.

Blakely has redefined the undergarment industry, through her groundbreaking Spanx products. She has been named the world's youngest, self-made female billionaire by Forbes Magazine and is one of TIME's 100 Most Influential People.

What does imperfect action look like in practice?

It meant having an idea and taking a pair of scissors to cut away her undergarments to create something better.

It meant researching and writing her own patent applications. Unable to afford the legal fees, she bought a book and did it herself.

Would a lawyer have done it better?

Yes of course, but it was good enough to get going.

It meant taking her body-contouring products to the real world before they were perfected to get live customer feedback to make them better.

It meant that instead of hiring models to advertise her products, she hired everyday women to be her brand ambassadors.

One story highlights her approach to not waiting for perfect.

She called the offices of important buyers over and over again. Her persistence led to one buyer agreeing to meet her for 10 minutes if she flew to Dallas.

A few minutes into the meeting, she knew she was losing them.

Her imperfect response was "I need you to come to the bathroom with me"

The buyer agreed.

In that bathroom, she demonstrated the power of Spanx by trying on that same pair of cream-coloured pants she had worn when she first invented the product, both with her invention and without it for comparison.

The buyer agreed to sell the product in seven of her stores.

Rules are meant to be broken.

Who defined the rules anyway? What made those rules right?

Is there a better way to do things?

A different way?

A less perfect way?

Challenge Yourself

If you're prone to getting stuck in a cycle of waiting for perfect, this is for you.

Some questions to ask yourself:

Why am I not taking action?

Reflect on what's going on? What is stopping you from taking action?

Is it a real reason or an imagined fear?

Is there a different way that you could think about what's stopping you?

What's the worst that could happen?

It's quite easy to catastrophise and create a range of scenarios that have nothing to do with the reality of where you are.

Really consider what is the worst-case scenario of your current worry.

More often than not, the imagined fear of a failed experiment or past memories of failed experiments are far greater than the reality of where you are.

See if you can quantify the downside risk.

If it's a business experiment, what's the very most that a failed experiment could cost you?

Would paying that price in the worst-case scenario help inform you and move you forward?

And what if it succeeds? What would the upside be?

Perfectionism is all too often driven by emotion rather than logic.

See if you can't cut through the emotion and uncover the cold, hard logic that decisions need.

Thoughtful Disagreement

Don't sit in silence.

Remember your number on the scale of 1-100.

Who has a different view to you?

If you're prone to perfectionism, find someone who is prone to action.

If you're prone to action, find someone who is prone to perfectionism.

Engage in thoughtful disagreement.

Push the boundaries of thought and challenge yourself to see what perspectives you are missing.

When we consider diverse points of view, we are more likely to make better decisions.

Better Decisions

Having a Big Bold Mindset is all about the path to taking better decisions.

Each action we take is an experiment to inform us as to what our next action could be.

In my business, the pain of perfectionism cost us the market leader position with that product.

That pain led us to reflect and adapt our approach.

We subsequently made some better decisions.

We innovated in a different direction and created a new product. We adapted what we had and created something new that then became the engine of our growth.

We listened.

We debated.

We adapted.

We made progress.

That's what the Big Bold Mindset does. It doesn't get stuck waiting for perfection.

Theme 5: Bigger Resilience

Despite the best preparation in the world, there will be times when the s**t hits the fan.

Guaranteed.

Should you leave your response to chance?

Or should you look to develop your resilience now, so that you're in the best place possible to ride the most challenging of storms.

It's time to explore what you and your team can do to become more resilient.

The next four chapters will show you how.

Use them to develop awareness, skills and tools to respond to the toughest challenges.

Let them help you develop bigger resilience.

Chapter 17 – Strengthen with Safety

The CEO of one 10,000-person strong company knew the issue and needed help, explaining:

We have a high-performance culture and our team are driven go-getters. We get great results BUT, we have a culture that is toxic.

We are struggling to adapt to changes in the market. Our challenge as an organisation is that we don't have a culture of owning mistakes. Accountability is not seen as a good thing.

This has created real problems. No-one wants to be seen as the person who failed. We're encouraging people to be reflective and own their mistakes. But no-one wants to.

The resistance to accountability has been huge. People have lied and hidden problems. Issues that we should have known about have not surfaced.

It's a toxic recipe.

We know as an organisation we have to change and we need to own our mistakes but it's just ingrained in our culture. As senior leaders, we know this is not sustainable.

Help!

My brief was to speak to their top 120 performers to help them through a transformation journey.

The journey from being a purely numbers-driven organisation to one that put people first and could become more reflective, more accountable, and more adaptive.

Without that accountability, it's incredibly hard to see the truth that the mistakes hid. This makes it near impossible to become a future-ready organisation.

An agile organisation that can adapt and change to an increasingly disrupted world.

It was a challenge I am more than familiar with.

Familiar because I have been on that exact same journey in my own life.

A journey to create agile teams that can adapt to changing conditions, who value growth and support each other instinctively.

What Lies Beneath the Surface?

Every behaviour is a form of communication.

The actions that an individual makes communicates information about that individual.

Likewise, the actions that an organisation takes communicates information about its culture.

It's in examining these behaviours that we can understand what is going on beneath the surface and start to make different choices.

What was going on beneath the surface here?

The message told me that people do not feel safe to own mistakes in this organisation.

It had a culture where showing any vulnerability was not ok.

A culture where people feel there will be ramifications if they speak the truth.

It's hard to see how this type of culture can be changed without strong leadership throughout.

Strong leadership with a clear set of messages and actions that are consistent.

Messages and actions where senior leaders lead by example with the type of culture they aspire to.

It requires leaders to face their own emotional blackspots.

To be open and vulnerable.

To own mistakes.

The only way to create that culture shift is for senior leaders to start with personal accountability and showing those traits consistently over time.

It's hard to do when vulnerability is not a part of the DNA of a company culture.

It's hard, but it's necessary.

Where Are You?

How safe do you feel to speak your truth at work?

Safe to share mistakes, vulnerabilities, and challenges?

On a scale of 1 to 100, where do you score?

What about at home or with friends?

How safe do you feel to be totally raw and open?

In truth, when I was working in the corporate world, I didn't score highly on this scale. This lack of safety resulted in my playing small, never really pushing the boundaries and developing the skills I needed as a leader at work.

At home I felt much safer and it was here I developed many of my leadership and skills needed for the Big Bold Mindset.

Once I had developed those skills at home, I was better prepared to utilise them in the workplace.

The Science of Safety

The term 'psychological safety' was coined by Amy Edmondson, Professor of Leadership and Management at Harvard Business School.

Edmondson defines psychological safety as a shared belief within a team or organisation that it is safe to take interpersonal risks, such as speaking up, expressing ideas, and asking questions without fear of negative consequences or judgement.

An environment where individuals feel comfortable being themselves, sharing their thoughts and feelings, and engaging in open and honest dialogue.

How does a lack of this show up in organisations with low psychological safety?

Fear of Speaking Up

Employees hesitate to share their thoughts and ideas. The fear of negative consequences, criticism, or retribution stifles open communication and hampers the free flow of information and creativity.

Lack of Trust

Trust is lacking or eroded among team members and between employees and leaders. There may be a sense of scepticism, suspicion, or a belief that mistakes will be harshly punished rather than seen as learning opportunities.

Blame Culture

Organisations with low psychological safety often have a blame culture, where mistakes are met with blame and finger-pointing rather than a focus on understanding and resolving issues. This can lead to a culture of fear and avoidance of taking risks.

Micromanagement

Leaders may micromanage employees, closely monitoring and controlling their work, which leaves little room for autonomy or creative problem-solving. This lack of autonomy stifles innovation and employee growth.

Lack of Collaboration

Team members may compete against each other rather than collaborating. Silos and departmental boundaries are common, inhibiting effective cross-functional teamwork and knowledge sharing.

Limited Feedback and Growth

Employees may receive limited or ineffective feedback, hindering their personal and professional development. There may be a lack of opportunities for learning and growth, leading to stagnation and disengagement.

Exclusion and Bias

Diversity and inclusion may be lacking, with limited representation of different perspectives and experiences. Discrimination, bias, and exclusionary practices may exist, creating an environment that is unwelcoming or hostile to certain groups.

Resistance to Change

There may be a resistance to change and new ideas, with a preference for maintaining the status quo. This resistance can hinder innovation and adaptation to evolving market demands.

These characteristics create an environment where employees feel unsupported, afraid to take risks, and hesitant to contribute their thoughts.

The reverse is also true.

Organisations where people feel psychologically safe have higher levels of trust, communication is open and honest with a focus on continuous learning and growth.

Leaders support growth and lead by example creating teams who are open to new ideas, embrace change, and encourage innovation. Teams where employees are encouraged to think creatively and contribute innovative solutions to challenges.

Find the Truth

The data is clear.

Research by MIT found that agile firms grow revenue 37% faster and generate 30% higher profits than non-agile firms.

MIT also found that teams who trust their leaders are 42 times more likely to be *highly resilient.*

In a world where disruption is the name of the game, organisations have no choice but to become more agile and resilient to be able to adapt to ever changing market conditions.

To adapt you need to hear the truth.

To hear the messages and adapt.

To unleash your very finest talent to get creative, to find new solutions.

That is a very tall order in a team where people aren't safe to speak their truth, to experiment, to learn and to grow.

It's literally an existential risk to organisations who are not prepared to make the changes needed.

Big Bold Leaders

Prior to Satya Nadella taking over as CEO of Microsoft in 2014, the once innovative and fast-moving organisation had been challenged.

Microsoft had developed a reputation for being a highly competitive and internally focused organisation.

A culture described as 'cut throat', where employees were ranked against each other and the focus was on individual performance rather than collaboration.

A culture that was often characterised as bureaucratic, hierarchical, and resistant to change.

A culture that had become risk-averse, with a fear of failure, which was stifling creativity and innovation, as employees were hesitant to take risks or challenge the status quo.

Nadella recognised the need for a cultural shift within the company to foster innovation, collaboration, and empathy.

His leadership style prioritised empathy and vulnerability.

An environment where employees would feel empowered to take risks, share their ideas, and collaborate more effectively.

He encouraged a growth mindset with employees embracing challenges, learning from failures, and valuing feedback.

He shared personal stories about his own failures and challenges, and how he had learned from them.

He encouraged employees to do the same, creating an environment where mistakes were seen as opportunities for growth rather than reasons for punishment.

The importance of diverse perspectives and experiences in driving innovation was encouraged.

By promoting diversity at all levels of the company, he created a culture where employees felt valued and included, which in turn fostered a sense of psychological safety and openness.

Microsoft's culture has gone through a transformation to one that prioritises empathy, vulnerability, and emotional intelligence.

This shift in culture has allowed the company to adapt to changing market dynamics, drive innovation, and attract top talent.

The numbers speak for themselves. Since his appointment, the market capitalisation has grown from $315 billion to $2,485 billion as of 2 June 2023 - an increase of over seven-fold.

Truly when you put people first, the results will follow.

The Journey to Safer

There are two journeys to creating teams where people feel safe.

The first is your personal journey. Something we will explore in the next chapter. It's hard to demonstrate and lead with vulnerability when we've not faced our own emotional blackspots.

The second is the collective journey for your team culture as a whole.

Some experiments for you to consider on your journey to creating a team where innovation, creativity and growth can thrive:

Lead from the front: Senior leaders from the CEO and Chair down need to set the tone.

Model vulnerability by sharing stories where you have been challenged and have found a path through it.

Demonstrate listening.

Value diverse perspectives.

In the team you work in, model the behaviours you want to see more of.

Praise and celebrate when you see others modelling these behaviours.

Raise awareness of new ways of thinking like the Growth Mindset.

Your team may include people for whom this is a totally new concept.

These ideas can take time to fully absorb and embrace.

Encourage open conversations.

Build trust by acting on what you hear.

Actively listen and respond to feedback.

Be patient.

Be consistent.

Don't expect change overnight.

Think like a farmer.

Imagine you are planting seeds and applying sunshine and water. If you plant seeds today and expect an oak tree tomorrow, the only person who is being deluded is you.

Creating a psychologically safe team is an ongoing process that requires commitment, continuous effort, and a willingness to adapt.

It is important to involve employees at all levels and empower them to contribute to the creation of a safe and inclusive work environment.

Unlock the Benefits

We are not thinking creatures who feel, we are feeling creatures who think.

To be human is to have emotions.

To take the time to understand our emotions, to master all too often the unspoken inner world is where the keys to the Big Bold Mindset sit.

At an organisation level, it's crucial to understand how our teams feel.

Creating that feeling of safety will unlock huge benefits.

What's the single biggest enabler of you being able to lead a psychologically safe organisation?

It's understanding your own emotional pathways and blackholes.

Chapter 18 – Master Your Emotions

As a senior leader the daily pressures can be relentless.

High expectations for continuous growth and no room for errors or setbacks

Employees needing help on how to navigate through uncertainty.

The responsibility for the team weighs heavily.

The need to balance well-being with the growth agenda.

Competitors waiting to pounce on any misstep.

Changing economic conditions bring complex trading environments and shifting consumer preferences.

Late nights and early mornings.

An endless stream of meetings, negotiations, and strategic planning.

Personal sacrifices as family, hobbies, and self-care take a backseat to the never-ending demands of the role.

The crucible of pressure as a senior leader is real.

These pressures show up in the data.

In 2022, 38 CEOs of FTSE 350 companies stood down[27].

Of the largest 350 companies listed in the UK Stock Exchange, more than 10% of their CEO's resigned in one year.

That is more than *double* what it was the previous year.

18 CEOs resigned in 2021 rising to 38 in 2022.

I suspect that if you asked those CEO's the previous year whether they were tough enough, resilient enough, my hunch is that every single one of them would have said they were.

It's a standard response, right?

Are you tough enough?

Resilient enough?

Or is there room to improve?

I truly believe that the standard advice and strategies around resilience are not working any more.

We are long overdue for a re-think of how we think about resilience.

To look again at what it means to be tough enough to withstand the pressures of being a senior leader today.

I used to think that being tougher meant setting your face against the wind and grinding it out day to day.

---

27 https://www.thecorporategovernanceinstitute.com/insights/news-analysis/ceos-are-burned-out-and-leaving/

The military and hero stories swirled in my mind of how mental toughness was just all about grit.
There is certainly a place for that.

But to only focus on that misses a huge and very important part of the story.

And that involves looking *inward* rather than *outward.*

That involves understanding our emotions.

Our patterns.

Our responses.

And doing the deep work on how we face the world.

Look Inward. Not Outward.

"Everyone has weaknesses which are revealed in the pattern of mistakes that they make. Knowing what your weaknesses are and staring hard at them is the first step on the path to success. Those who don't see them or acknowledge their weaknesses are doomed to be crippled by them".

The words of Ray Dalio.

Not the usual words you'd expect to hear from someone who has built a world class financial services company about the importance of staring inwards and recognising what our patterns are.

The challenge with the 'toughing it out' approach, a message that feels omnipresent, is that when we tough it out, when we set our face against the wind, we close down our time for introspection.

The time for exploring those repeating patterns.

The irony I believe is that by cultivating a workforce based only on 'toughing it out', is that we are creating weaker workforces.

Creating cultures that are less resilient.

Not more.

To have a Big Bold Mindset is to take on a different way of thinking.

And right at the core of that is better understanding the human animal.

You are either the master of your emotions.

Or they are the master of you.

Where you are the puppet reacting with emotions to each situation that arises.

Exhausted and drained, as those emotions play out.

The same issues repeat time and again until you reach burnout.

The choice is threefold:

1. Think smaller and keep things at the same level or reduce what you do.

2. Keep pressing on until you burn out.

3. Learn to master your emotions.

Candid Self Disclosure

It took me many years to face the truth of my own mistakes and weaknesses.

Emotional patterns that I developed early in my life played out for far too long in my adult life.

Three particular patterns stood out for me in the past:

Ego

I'm right and you're wrong. All the behaviours and actions I took had to point to the fact that I was right and all too often at the expense of other people.

Blame

It's your fault. Not mine. Not taking ownership of when things went wrong. Being ashamed of getting the wrong answer and doing everything I could to avoid being exposed or embarrassed in this position.

Victim

This was a particularly pernicious one as it stayed hidden from me for a long time. It was the notion that things are being done to me and that I'm helpless and a victim in each challenging situation.

I no longer fight against these patterns.

The pain of staring at your weaknesses is, in my experience, more than happily compensated for the moment I realised that I am no longer at their mercy.

When I was able to tell the story of it and no longer be impacted by it.

When I could see situations playing out and I didn't have the same response that I once did.

We all have our ingrained emotional patterns.

All of us.

No matter where we are in the world.

No matter how senior or junior we are.

The fact that we have ingrained emotional responses is a core defining feature of being a human.

Your emotional patterns will be unique to you.

Shaped by your life experiences.

It's your choice as to whether you want to explore them.

Where Are You?

How self-aware are you of your emotional patterns and responses?

When you are under pressure, which is when these patterns most show up, what are your defaults?

What is the emotional home that you go to?

Right now, grab a pen and paper, making note of some of the patterns that you are aware of.

If you reflect, do you see the same patterns playing out time and again?

How we do anything is how we do everything, so the patterns will reveal themselves when we take the time to look for them.

We can use a simple example to highlight why it's so important to reflect and look for them.

Right now.

Look around wherever you are. Scan around with your eyes and notice how many items are red in colour.

Take 30 seconds and count up how many different red items you can see.

Done that?

Ok good.

How many green items did you see?

Probably none or very few right?

When we instruct our brains to look for things, we usually find them.

When we don't instruct our brains to look for things, we seldom see them.

Take a look now.

What repeating emotional patterns can you find? I have some practical tools for you later on this.

The Science of Emotions

Harvard Business School Professor Linda Hill believes leaders must engage with emotions more than ever.[28]

Part of her 2022 research involved surveying 1,500 executives globally and running round tables with over 200 executives.

---

[28] https://hbr.org/2022/03/hbs-professor-linda-hill-says-leaders-must-engage-with-emotions-as-never-before

When leaders were asked what skills they needed to lead right now, the top four were adaptability, curiosity, creativity, and comfort with ambiguity.

All skills that require sitting with high levels of uncertainty.

Skills that are more likely to trigger higher emotional states.

Hill focuses on the evolving role of leaders in the modern workplace and in particular the need to effectively navigate the emotional landscape.

She found that traditional leadership approaches often focused on rationality and downplayed emotions.

In today's complex and dynamic work environments, leaders must acknowledge and address emotions to foster collaboration, innovation, and employee well-being.

Hill suggests that leaders should start by embracing their own emotions.

When leaders do this, they are more likely to create a psychologically safe environment that fosters open communication and trust.

An approach that allows teams to collectively navigate challenges, share diverse perspectives, and enhance problem-solving capabilities.

Stuck in the Past

You can't solve the problems of today using solutions of the past.

As the resignation data shows, we need fresh solutions.

The breakthroughs from the work of psychologists like Bessel van der Kolk and Gabor Maté have shown us very clear science that points to understanding our emotions in ways that are new.

These new approaches need to be understood, reflected on, and integrated into how leaders operate.

The single best way to start is with yourself.

It's nigh on impossible to help guide others through highly charged emotional states unless leaders themselves have confronted their own emotional blackholes.

The risk of ignoring science breakthroughs and the skills needed is the very real risk of burnout, both individually and with the teams that work within them.

Big Bold Leaders

Jeff Weiner, the former CEO of LinkedIn, is a leader who embraces vulnerability and emotional awareness.

During his tenure, Weiner openly discussed his personal experiences with burnout, stress, and the importance of well-being.

He believed that acknowledging and addressing emotions in the workplace was crucial for building a healthy and productive organisational culture.

Weiner prioritised transparency and vulnerability, often sharing personal stories during company wide meetings and during interviews.

By sharing his own challenges and vulnerabilities, Weiner created a safe space for employees to do the same.

An approach that fosters trust, authenticity, and a sense of psychological safety.

He also emphasises the importance of compassion and empathy in leadership.

At LinkedIn, he implemented programs encouraging employees to bring their whole selves to work, recognising that emotional well-being directly impacts performance.

He is not alone.

Weiner is one of a growing number of leaders who recognise that the way we lead needs to evolve.

We're all a Work In Progress

I have a simple formula. It's called the WIP or Work in Progress formula.

Weakness + Introspection = Progress.

None of us are the finished article.

We all have room for growth and improvement.

No matter where you are in your career there is always space for more.

The formula has three steps:

Step 1 - Identify your weaknesses

First, reflect on your own repeating patterns and challenges.

Can you see a common thread that runs through there? Ask yourself the question and make notes in a dedicated notebook.

Think about times when you've been challenged.

What happened?

What did you do?

Look for the patterns.

Secondly, you need to ask for feedback from people who you trust.

Be candid and open.

Share that you are looking for ways to grow and develop.

Ask for their views on what your single biggest weakness is.

This can be challenging.

Think of it like peeling back layers of an onion.

There are almost certainly many layers and probably a few tears as you peel back each skin.

Here's the cold-hard truth.

Other people can so often see us much better than we see ourselves.

To prove this, just think of people you know well.

Could you easily pinpoint what their single biggest weakness is?

Something that they do which you are fairly certain is holding them back?

My hunch is that after a brief reflection you could find something insightful and valuable to share with a number of people that you know well.

And it will be the same with people who know you well.

Ask the question.

And then write down whatever they say.

Don't argue or overthink it.

Just write it down and ask for more clarification if that would help.

How you react to this feedback is crucial.

Here's why.

We don't normally have this conversation.

People aren't used to giving feedback like this.

Chances are that people who know you well won't want to hurt your feelings so they may go "light" on the feedback at first to see how you react.

If you react badly, it's very unlikely they will go deeper and give you more feedback.

And it's going deeper and getting that feedback that is where that truth will sit.

The feedback is a gift and you want to take and then move to the next step.

Step 2 - Introspection

You've now got some notes.

Notes of your own and feedback from one or more people on your single biggest weakness.

You've now got to sit with this.

This is the part that separates those who really want a bigger bold mindset and those who don't.

It separates people because it's painful.

It's painful because it means staring at our own inadequacies.

As you think about it, start to think about what you can do differently.

Awareness is the first step to change.

The first big emotional black hole that I had was blame.

I wrote the word blame in large letters on an A4 sheet of paper.

I stuck it on the mirror in my bathroom.

I chose to get irritated by it.

To let it get under my skin.

To keep it front of mind so that I could make different choices.

To think of different situations where in the past I would have blamed someone.

Now, I was thinking "how can I take more responsibility and do something that will help this situation. What can I personally and specifically do differently?".

Step 3 - Progress

Become aware of what you do in pressure situations.

Watch how your responses change.

Make notes and acknowledge when you make a different set of choices to ones that you would have done before.

Acknowledge that this is hard and you are pulling out the roots of emotional patterns that have been shaped over a lifetime.

Keep going.

The Never-Ending Journey

This is a journey that has its own rewards.

The reward is the removal of the repeating patterns that you once had and replacing them with healthier responses.

As with every idea in this book, there are two levels you can approach this. With the cognitive technique you've just read about. And the beyond cognitive techniques that we covered earlier.

This journey is not for the faint of heart. It's only one that seriously ambitious leaders who want to make a difference will embark upon because it's tough.

The uninformed will tend to traditional mental toughness techniques and grit it out on the surface.

Those who find it too tough will swerve it and likely seek smaller less threatening goals.

And those who seek bigger and bolder things will embrace their weaknesses with both hands and find better ways to navigate them.

The choice is yours.

Chapter 19 – Calculate Your Risks

Stick with the status quo or take a bold step into the unknown?

Sitting at the dinner table she had zoned out while listening to her children speaking. She was weighing up which step to take next. It's all she could think of.

It was a pivotal moment and there were no certainties.

Only unanswered questions.

Over the past few years, the business had experienced strong growth.

The pressure to maintain that growth weighed heavily on her.

And the market was changing fast. New technologies flooding the market.

A changing economic and political landscape.

As CEO, she questioned herself.

Did she have the vision and capabilities to lead in these uncertain times?

On the side of the coin was a deep sense of urgency to push the boundaries, to innovate, to drive change.

The opportunity to seize the market and take the initiative. To become the market leader.

The team to really make a difference. The team that talent gravitates towards.

The pull to be bold was strong.

So was the fear of getting it wrong.

The fear of missing the moment, of being the laggard as the sector embraced new technology and a changing market was massive.

There were loud voices at the board room urging faster innovation.

Move too slowly and risk stagnation.

Talent departing for the nimble renegades disrupting the market.

Get it wrong and over-invest was an existential threat.

It meant risking much of what had been created.

It's a decision every ambitious leader will almost certainly face multiple times in their career.

Do you take the leap or play it safe?

Is the safe option really that safe?

What's the Real Risk?

While ensuring you don't wait for perfection, how can you consider the risks? As humans, how well do we really understand and evaluate risks?

What is the role of critical thinking versus emotion in terms of how we make choices and move through uncertainty?

Do you throw caution to the wind?

Do you get analysis paralysis and so lost in information you can no longer see the wood for the trees?

A simple example to illustrate how clouded human judgement becomes when we face situations with risk.

Which of the following do you perceive as high risk?

- Shark Attacks
- Road Accidents
- Unhealthy Diet

Here's the statistics for each of those three areas:

Shark Attacks - 10 people killed a year.

The risk of being killed by a shark is extremely low. According to the International Shark Attack File, the average number of fatal shark attacks worldwide is estimated to be around 10 per year.

Road Accidents - 1.35 million people a year

Road accidents pose a much higher risk compared to shark attacks. According to the World Health Organization (WHO), road traffic accidents are a major cause of death worldwide. Globally, approximately 1.35 million people die in road accidents each year.

Unhealthy Diet - 11 million people a year

Poor diet and lifestyle choices can contribute to various health problems, including chronic diseases such as heart disease, diabetes, and certain types of cancer. The World Health Organization estimates that unhealthy diets contribute to approximately 11 million deaths annually worldwide.

Would you have guessed the right order and more importantly the magnitude of the differences.

We don't think of poor diet when we do our grocery shopping in the same way as we think of shark attacks and imagine the film, Jaws.

The point is this.

As humans we experience a range of biases which mean we don't see risk clearly.

We get clouded by emotion.

We don't engage in critical thinking.

Because of a lack of critical thinking, we don't take the steps needed to explore and minimise what risks there may be that could lead to radically different outcomes.

We scratch research and go with our gut, a gut that may be wrong.

Where Are You?

How good is your decision making?

Do you use any techniques to evaluate how good your decisions in the past have been?

How do you use those feedback loops to inform your next set of decisions?

How aware of biases are you?

The Science of Bias

Biased thinking is the tendency of the human mind to make judgments or reach conclusions in a way that is influenced by preconceived notions, prejudices, or personal beliefs, rather than actually seeing the truth of the situation.

We talked briefly about this in Chapter 1, when we examined the past, present, and future biassed perspectives we all have.

To fully engage a Big Bold Mindset is to become more aware of those biases.

If we don't become aware of those biases, we run the very real risk of avoiding choices that in reality have a significantly lower risk that we might at first perceive.

And of course, the opposite is true. That we might make choices that have a seemingly low risk but in reality, are laden with risks hidden from an initial glance.

Shining a light on our human decision making.

Nobel prize winner, Daniel Kahneman has spent a career shining a light on the psychology of judgement and decision making. In his groundbreaking book, *Thinking Fast and Slow,* he details a number of biases.

Some of the biases I see commonly showing up that impact our ability to have a Big Bold Mindset include:

Confirmation Bias

This is a tendency to only seek out information that proves what we already believe to be true. We only see evidence that supports our hypothesis. We ignore or downplay information that contradicts our beliefs.

Remember the last chapter and the experiment to count the number of red items? We don't see green things when we are not looking for them.

In a business context, when you are seeking to think bigger and bolder, the bias to only see and hear things that support your existing point of view only can be fatal.

There are times when we take a position for emotional reasons and we set ourselves up to defend that position. It takes humility and courage to stand back and look at those emotional reasons and to ask ourselves if we are right to take that stance.

Anchoring Bias

This is a tendency to place too much emphasis on the first piece of information we hear on a subject.

Experienced salespeople know this well and early on in a negotiation will seek to anchor a very high price in their prospect's minds.

When it comes to decision making, it can be hard to undo the effect of this anchor, even in the face of contradictory information.

Who watched Jaws many years ago and still think of shark attacks when they go swimming in the sea, despite the fact that you're more likely to be killed while driving to the beach?

One startup venture I am involved in is being impacted by a situation exactly like this. Our product is a UV light solution to kill pathogens inside building ventilation systems. It has been proven to be safe through rigorous scientific testing and accreditation.

At one potential customer meeting, an important decision maker had a harmful experience with UV many years ago. Despite the solution being proven to be totally safe, there has been significant resistance to the solution.

What beliefs are you holding about the decisions that you face right now? How significant is the first piece of information you had versus subsequent information?

Loss Aversion Bias

This is the tendency to strongly prefer avoiding losses over acquiring equivalent gains.

It is a cognitive bias where people place more emphasis on the potential negative outcomes rather than the potential positive outcomes.

For them, the pain of losing something is psychologically more significant than the pleasure of gaining something of equal value.

This is especially relevant to the Big Bold Mindset as it makes people more likely to be hesitant in taking risks due to the fear of potential losses.

Availability Bias

This is the bias that occurs when individuals assess the likelihood of an event based on how easily they can recall similar instances from memory.

In business, this can lead to an overemphasis on recent or highly publicised risks, while neglecting less memorable but equally important risks.

Overconfidence Bias

This is where people overestimate their own abilities and the accuracy of their predictions. This bias can result in excessive risk-taking or a failure to adequately assess potential risks and uncertainties.

These are just a sample of the biases to become aware of.

The good news is that once we become aware of the biases which we are all fallible to, we can take positive steps to negate them.

Big Bold (AI) Leaders

We live in a world of AI, of Machine Learning where new innovation is being rolled out daily. Our new world has much to teach us.

The story of one of the earliest innovations in this field shines a light on how machines think of risk as compared to humans.

On March 9, 2016, the worlds of Go and artificial intelligence collided in South Korea for an extraordinary best-of-five-game competition, coined The DeepMind Challenge Match[29].

Go is a board game of immense complexity and strategic depth.

[29]https://www.youtube.com/watch?v=WXuK6gekU1Y

Hundreds of millions of people around the world watched as a legendary Go master, Lee Sedol took on an unproven AI challenger for the first time in history.

There is a fascinating moment in the film, Google DeepMind Challenge Match which is freely available to watch on YouTube.

It is when the AI challenger, DeepMind, makes a series of moves that make no sense to the experts watching.

You can see the best player in the world Lee Sedol confused by the moves.

A set of moves that no human would make.

A set of moves that seem destined to lose the game.

A set of moves that ended with Deep Mind winning the game.

It's a fascinating insight into how cold hard logic wins.

The AI can think many moves further ahead than the human brain.

The human brain is limited in its capacity to think so many moves ahead.

The AI is virtually unlimited.

It's about how logic can triumph over the human brain.

In your business, in your decision making, you will struggle to out-think an AI.

But you can out-think and out-manoeuvre other humans?

That requires the use of cold hard logic.

You need to make better decisions than your competitors.

There are plenty of examples of successful business leaders who explore all the risks and make the best decisions with what they have.

The process is the same.

The Devil is in the Detail

There is no substitute for critical thinking and deep research to come to your own conclusions. Your situation is unique to you and it requires your thinking, not the results of someone else's thinking.

There is nothing in life that is risk free.

If we avoided all risks, you'd never leave the house.

Some ideas on how to embrace risks and take bigger bolder decisions.

Become Self-Aware

Be aware that you will have many biases acting upon you. Have humility at hand to accept that you may be wrong.

Seek Diverse Perspectives

Actively seek out diverse opinions and viewpoints. Engaging with people who have different backgrounds and perspectives can challenge our biases and provide a broader range of insights to consider.

Reflect and Deliberate

Where you can, slow down and allow time for a more deliberate and thoughtful evaluation of options, reducing the likelihood of impulsive or biased choices.

Use Frameworks

Employ structured decision-making frameworks to minimise the influence of biases. Set criteria and systematically evaluate options.

Run Experiments

Where you can run as many experiments as possible to quickly test assumptions and gather data points. In an uncertain world, real world evidence can be the best guide as to our next actions.

Stay Open to Criticism

Encourage a culture of constructive criticism where people feel comfortable questioning assumptions and challenging biases. Constructive criticism and open discussions can help uncover blind spots and enhance decision-making.

Learn Fast

The only real competitive advantage any team has is their speed of learning and the ability to adapt. After making a decision, take the time to reflect on the outcomes and evaluate how biases may have influenced the process. Learn from any mistakes or biases that may have occurred and use those experiences to improve future decision-making.

Take Ownership

When we sailed as a family team many people thought we were crazy.

Many still do.

We did the thinking and years of preparation to find ways to mitigate every single risk we could imagine.

Painstaking research and actions.

We listed every single risk.

We held each risk up to the light.

Was it a real risk or an imagined risk?

What are the percentage chances of that risk actually happening?

What steps can we take to mitigate that risk?

What resources and training can we take?

Only when we have thoroughly evaluated every single risk and had gotten comfortable with that did we decide to proceed.

What decisions are you facing?

List out the options.

List out the risks.

Engage critical thinking.

Those with a Big Bold Mindset refuse to accept dogma which is the result of other people's thinking. They choose to do their own thinking, their own research and reach their own conclusions.

Sometimes this looks like doing things which everyone else will think is crazy.

Provided you've done your own thinking, pulled apart the biases and applied your own cold hard logic, bet on yourself. Not in a throw caution to the wind way. But in a way that is grounded and has been built from the bottom up with careful consideration and logic.

Chapter 20 – Create Through Conflict

There were strong voices around the table.

And quiet voices around the table.

The problems in the business were clear to see, but they needed fresh ideas to solve them.

This was a time when everyone would need to step forward, to contribute.

No point in having lots of talent and that talent not showing up.

The CEO noticed that when it got heated, some people hated the conflict and withdrew.

It started a thought process.

What is the relationship that each person has with conflict?

Some people seem to thrive on it.

Some people seem to run from it.

What was the difference and what could be done differently.

One answer was around creating psychological safety. That was the overall outcome as a culture.

But what about the mindset?

Diving deeper, what was going on for each person.

Once a spotlight was shone on it, it was apparent that it showed up in other ways too: a reluctance to have the tough conversations; sugar coating the truth to avoid conflict; and staying at surface level rather than getting into the depth of issues.

These behaviours would take the team further away from the goal, not closer.

" What could be done to explore this issue, and find better solutions?"

Grappling with the Issue

The Harvard Business Review in May 2023[30] in an article on *Why Conflicting Ideas Can Make Your Strategy Stronger,* suggests that in order to succeed in a volatile, uncertain world, successful strategies require managers to develop better skills around the idea of conflict.

Skills that embrace incompatible and misaligned ideas.

Skills that communicate multiple and conflicting narratives.

Skills that mean that they share ideas as they think of them as opposed to the traditional sequence of thinking then sharing.

This means leaders and managers have to embrace conflict.

---

30 https://hbr.org/2023/05/why-conflicting-ideas-can-make-your-strategy-stronger?ab=HP-hero-latest-text-1

Having a Big Bold Mindset means that ambitious leaders need to better understand the relationship we all have with conflict.

Leaders need to be able foster a culture in which people can disagree without being punished for it.

That understanding to struggle better and embrace conflicting points of view is essential when dealing with hard problems that will come up along the way to achieving big bold goals.

Where Are You?

I'd like you to do a very broad and crude experiment.

Reflect on your own relationship with conflict.

Do you run towards or away from it?

It's likely that the answer will be nuanced.

Situation dependent and person dependent.

It might be different at work and at home.

It might vary from person to person.

For the purpose of this experiment, it's about just getting a sense and opening the door to better conversations around conflict.

Let's try a very rough quantification, a set of numbers that can open the door to think about it in a different way.

Think of your own relationship with conflict.

What is your natural tendency, your default state around conflict.

If you had to rate how comfortable you are with each of these three states in relation to conflict, where might it sit?

Hate it

Neutral

Love it

An example to illustrate:

10-10-80 - most of the time I'm very happy embracing conflict.

15-70-15 - I'm pretty much in the middle, I can go either way.

90-10-0 - I really hate conflict. I know I need to embrace it, but it makes me very uncomfortable.

What would your numbers be?

What would they be for others in your team at work and at home?

Why might this crude and imprecise question be helpful?

One feature of the human animal is a tendency towards centre of the world thinking.

We put ourselves at the centre of our world and because we think one way, we tend to assume that other people think the same way.

Having this conversation with others makes us more aware that this just isn't the case.

It enables us to appreciate other perspectives.

It enables us to better understand ourselves and others.

It can open the door to better conversations.

The Science of Conflict

Researchers have uncovered a wide range of reasons why we might have different relationships with conflict.

At a high level, some reasons include:

Personal experiences

Our past experiences with conflict play a crucial role in shaping our attitudes and responses. Positive experiences, such as successfully resolving conflicts or using conflict as an opportunity for growth, may lead to a more positive outlook on conflict. Conversely, negative experiences, like unresolved or escalated conflicts, can create fear, avoidance, or hostility towards conflict.

Personality traits

Individual differences in personality traits can influence how we approach and handle conflict. For example, individuals who are naturally assertive or competitive may embrace conflict and see it as an opportunity to assert themselves or achieve their goals. In contrast, individuals who are more avoidant or accommodating may feel uneasy with conflict and prefer to maintain harmony.

Cultural and societal influences

Cultural and societal norms, values, and expectations can shape our perspectives on conflict. Different cultures may have varying beliefs about the appropriateness of open conflict, direct communication styles, or the role of hierarchy in conflict resolution. These cultural differences can influence our comfort level and strategies when dealing with conflict.

Communication and conflict resolution skills

Our ability to communicate effectively and navigate conflicts plays a significant role in our relationship with conflict. Individuals with strong communication and conflict resolution skills may view conflict as an opportunity for dialogue, growth, and problem-solving. On the other hand, those lacking these skills may perceive conflict as threatening or challenging to manage.

Beliefs and Values

Our beliefs and values influence our relationships with conflict. Individuals who value collaboration, empathy, and compromise may approach conflict with a mindset focused on finding common ground and building relationships. Others who prioritise personal rights, justice, or standing up for their principles may engage in conflict more confrontationally.

Emotional Intelligence

Emotional intelligence, including self-awareness, self-regulation, empathy, and social skills, can impact how we perceive and handle conflict. High emotional intelligence allows individuals to manage their emotions, understand other people's perspectives, and find constructive solutions during conflict. Conversely, low emotional intelligence may result in heightened emotional reactions or difficulties in understanding and addressing the underlying issues.

Personal Development

The extent to which we have done work on our own personal development to understand how we react. Our relationship with conflict can absolutely change and evolve over time depending on how much work we are prepared to do.

There is a huge amount of research and science that sits behind this.

For the purpose of this book, the key point to note is that once we become aware of our own relationship with conflict, we then have a choice.

A choice as to whether to evolve our relationship with conflict.

Many of the ideas in this book point to techniques such as cognitive based approaches like self-reflection, learning and the development of new skills, and beyond cognitive approaches.

Once we have faced our relationship with conflict, we are better able to understand, support and coach others in our teams.

Wasted Potential

In our teams how much of the huge human potential is wasted?
Wasted because we don't ask the hard questions.

Wasted because we don't create the time to answer the hard questions.

The Big Bold Mindset leaves no stone unturned on a quest to solve hard problems.

If we aren't able to unleash the full talents of our teams due to differing conflict dynamics, that is a big problem.

It makes a mockery of taking the time and energy to assemble a world class team of individuals.

It means we are much less likely to achieve our goals.

No stone unturned.

That is the way the Big Bold Mindset works.

Don't let your best talent not show up because you've not done the work to understand the very real features of the human animal.

Big Bold Leaders

Indra Nooyi served as the CEO of PepsiCo from 2006 to 2018 and was widely respected for her leadership style and business acumen.

Nooyi was faced with a choice between continuing with historically profitable product lines like soda and chips or innovating and bringing in new product lines.[31]

Consumer eating and drinking habits change over time and despite resistance, her job was to offer a broader range of healthier products while reducing the environmental impact of the company's operations.

---

31 https://www.gsb.stanford.edu/insights/pepsi-ceo-break-past-dont-play-too-nice

One of her most controversial initiatives[32] was to redirect Pepsi's considerable corporate spend away from junk foods and into healthier alternatives.

Nooyi reclassified Pepsi's wide-ranging products into three categories, designed to give customers more information about the foods they consume:

- 'fun for you' (such as potato chips and regular soda).

- 'better for you' (diet or low-fat versions of snacks and fizzy drinks), and

- 'good for you' (for example, the recently acquired Quaker Oats oatmeal).

In 2010, she declared that Pepsi needed to be part of the solution to "one of the world's biggest public health challenges – a challenge fundamentally linked to our industry: obesity".

Under Nooyi's steer, Pepsi has reduced the portion sizes of its 'fun for you' products and has delivered a marketing campaign to ensure its 'diet' products are promoted as aspirationally as its full-sugar equivalents.

For example, the sports drink Gatorade, is now marketed specifically towards athletes, rather than being advertised as an everyday recreational beverage.

It was a classic example of needing to struggle well and take an entire organisation on a journey to stay in step with a marketplace demanding change.

Nooyi's approach to conflict was a key tenet of this.

---

[32] https://www.worldfinance.com/special-reports/how-indra-nooyi-changed-the-face-of-pepsico

She believed in fostering a collaborative and inclusive work environment and was known for her ability to navigate complex situations.

She prioritised open communication and encouraged constructive dialogue among employees.

She emphasised the value of diverse perspectives and believed that disagreements could lead to innovative solutions if managed effectively.

By shaping an environment where conflicts were addressed respectfully and productively, Nooyi created a culture where employees felt comfortable expressing their opinions without fear of backlash.

It was not about ignoring or suppressing conflicts but rather about finding ways to address them in a constructive manner.

Conflict is inevitable. It's about how you manage it.

Her approach showed what can be achieved through empathy, diplomacy, and a commitment to finding common ground.

During her 12-year stint as CEO, PepsiCo saw its revenue grow by more than 80 per cent and added a new billion-dollar brand almost every other year.

Nooyi trebled spending on R&D and focused on delivering sustainable long-term growth while leaving a more positive imprint on society and the environment.

Reflection, Feedback and Action

It starts with a personal journey.

A journey to understand our own relationship with conflict.

Step 1 - Self Reflection

Reflect on your past experiences with conflict.

Bring to mind sometimes when you have experienced it.

What did you do?

Focus more on what you did than what others did. This is the piece you have more control over.

What are the patterns and themes that you can see?

What impact did it have on those around you?

How did you resolve that conflict?

What could you have done differently?

Self-reflection can provide valuable insights into your relationship with conflict and help identify areas for personal growth.

Step 2 - Ask for Feedback

Ask trusted friends, family members, or colleagues for feedback on how you engage in conflict.

When they share ideas, do ask for clarification and examples, but don't argue!

Write them down to enable you to reflect on them.

The observations and insights from others can provide a different perspective on your conflict behaviours and help you gain a better understanding of how you come across to others during conflicts.

Step 3 - Pick one Thing

Of all the ideas and reflections, choose one thing to work on and develop.

It could be journaling strong emotions, it could be a training course, it could be therapy, it could be reframing consciously how you think about conflict.

Run some experiments.

See how this approach works.

Does it help or hinder?

Does it lead to better conversations where you go deeper in grappling with the hard problems?

Assess how this experiment worked and then devise the next experiment to try.

Grapple Forward

Strategy is no longer a single, unchanging roadmap. It's a portfolio of possibilities that requires an altogether new playbook.

Leaders must embrace the incompatibility and misalignment of ideas.

We must embrace conflict more.

We each have a different relationship with conflict.

A relationship shaped by our life experiences.

There are no classes at school that teach us how to handle conflict and how to struggle well to solve hard problems.

The Big Bold Mindset has to develop a healthier relationship with conflict.

This is an ongoing process that requires self-reflection, practice, and continuous learning.

Be patient with yourself and embrace opportunities for growth and self-improvement.

Be prepared for the grapple, the struggle with the hard problems as a team and embrace the conflict.

The Final Step

Chapter 21 – Adventure Beyond the Cognitive

Thinking on its own is not enough.

Those in pursuit of a bigger bolder mindset will want to leave no stone unturned.

And it's this final stone that for some may be the key to unlocking all the ideas we have built on so far.

The final step that goes deeper into how we as humans truly work.

First an important caveat. I'm not a psychologist, a doctor or a scientist.

The insights I share here are ones I have gleaned both from studying in this area, from my own personal experiences and from the various startups I am working with in the Mental Health space led by highly experienced clinicians.

I offer these insights as potential lines of inquiry for you to consider and to the thought leaders who are shining a light into this field.

I should further warn you that what I'm about to share with you may be seen by some as controversial.

Especially when it's in a book about mindset.

Mindset is typically referred to as how we think about things.

It focuses very much on what I'll refer to as our cognitive faculties.

Many of the ideas in this book we have covered are in the realm of our cognitive faculties.

How we think.

And at the same time, this is only part of the story.

The other part of the story for me goes beyond cognitive into the 'executive centre' of our brain, our in-built threat-detector that keeps us safe, guiding us away from danger through automatic responses.

It's about how we feel and what we can do to change that.

Neuroscientist Anthony Damasio elegantly summarises it as this: "We are not *thinking* creatures who feel, we are *feeling* creatures who think."

This is the journey to really understanding why we do what we do as humans.

If the answer to all our challenges was simply a cognitive one, then we would take all the advice out there and achieve our goals, our ambitions without much difficulty.

The hard truth is that it's much more complex than that.

We're humans, not machines.

We get derailed by these automatic responses.

We get derailed by our emotions.

We all know that if we want to get fit and healthy, we need to exercise and have the right diet.

Despite cognitively knowing this, how many people struggle to hit health and fitness goals?

This is but one example of why it's important to understand the impact of going beyond cognitive to achieve our goals.

This chapter will teach you about what it takes to do that when it comes to cracking mindset shifts. By the end of it, you'll have a choice.

Option A

To focus purely on the cognitive mindset ideas, that may or may not stick.

Option B

To explore why you sometimes sabotage your own progress, what you can do about it, and how you can then apply the 20 cognitive mindset shifts contained in this book with confidence.

There is no question in my mind that you will more rapidly accelerate towards a *sustainable* Big Bold Mindset using Option B.

For now, all I'd ask is to keep an open mind, to be curious and to consider what experiments you can run and explore this for yourself and find out what works for you.

My Journey Beyond Cognitive

Through my twenties and early thirties, if anyone suggested to me to talk to a psychologist, therapist, or psychiatrist, I'd have rolled my eyes and said, "I'm good thanks, I don't need a shrink".

It would have been an admission of failure, an admission that something was wrong with me.

By my late thirties, I was the co-founder of a tech startup that wasn't doing what I wanted it to do.

Which was to grow fast and make me lots of money that would make me happy.

It was doing completely the opposite of those three things and it was having the unfortunate side effect of souring my marriage at the same time.

I got stuck.

It finally reached the point where I got a business coach. This didn't feel as scary as a therapist but was pretty much the same thing.

That started a journey involving therapy, coaching, and counselling over a decade and a half.

A phrase really stuck in my mind that kept me sticking with it which was:" *The single biggest chokehold on any business is the psychology of its leaders."*

There is no doubt that the work that I was doing was helping and creating some awareness but I always had a nagging feeling there was something missing.

Caspar, You Do Know There's More Than Talk Therapy, Right?

Lis was calm, polite, and direct with a single question that completely wrongfooted me.

I was driving down the M4 motorway heading west from London on the way to our mastermind meeting.

I was now in my late 40s and was sharing a particular frustration I had at home with my wife Nichola. Something that had been causing me one too many sleepless nights. Like a stone in my shoe, it was an ever present irritant that I couldn't find a solution to.

I had been speaking monthly for several years with what I now understand is called a 'talk therapist' and it just didn't seem to be making any difference.

Lis is a highly respected expert in the field of mental health, having experienced considerable trauma herself early in life. If anyone knew about mindset and wellbeing, it was Lis.

Her language confused me.

I asked her what she meant.

She elaborated that traditional talk therapy is where you simply talk through the issues you're facing with a qualified expert.

The challenge is that pretty much everything stays in the realm of the cognitive and doesn't really go deep enough to make any difference to the things that really drive us and sit at a physical level in the body.

To be honest with you, I wasn't sure I really understood what she meant, but I was in a frustrated place, she was an expert with real credibility, and I was desperate enough to do something different.

That one question began a journey that changed everything.

The Trouble with Thinking

Try as we might to resolve life challenges at a cognitive level with either 'thinking techniques' or 'talk therapy', from what I have since experienced, seen and read, I believe without a shadow of doubt that the key to unlocking our potential is held in the body, not just the mind.

Thanks to the bestselling books of doctors such as Bessel van Der Kolk and Gabor Maté, I discovered just what is holding so many of us back from fully embodying our true potential: trauma.

You might be forgiven for wondering why I am bringing the notion of trauma in this book, a book for ambitious leaders.

Here's why:

In his life-changing book *The Body Keeps the Score*, van der Kolk says: "*Trauma is not what happens to us, it is what happens inside us.*"

The term trauma might be more helpfully explained as a 'defining emotional experience' that leaves a lasting imprint on us.

A lasting imprint that shapes all our behaviours going forward.

If we truly want to reshape these behaviours, we need to go deeper into understanding why we do what we do.

I can't think of a single person who doesn't regularly run into emotional black holes with the way they feel about challenging life events and the self-sabotaging behaviours that arise when they do.

I also can't think of a single person who hasn't had some kind of 'defining emotional experience' at some point in life.

Where Are You?

Can you recall strong emotional experiences from your life?

Perhaps, you, like me, were bullied at school.

Perhaps, you, like me, had parents who argued a lot,and in my case divorced.

Perhaps you had an experience that was frightening. I can remember being a toddler and having a large Alsatian jump up at me.

You will have your own experiences unique to you.

You don't have to go to war to experience strong emotions.

A simple thought experiment:

Imagine defining experiences on a scale of 1 to 100 in terms of the emotional impact they have on you.

Perhaps if you had been in a war, you might for example rate that as 90. That of course is a significant emotional experience.

Perhaps having a large dog jump up at you might rate as a 10.

Or some other experience might rate as a 30.

If you spoke to my mum, she'd view trauma as being binary. It's zero or one.

You've been at war and been traumatised.

Or it's nothing at all.

That clearly makes no sense and in reality, it is a sliding scale.

The experiences we have in life leave an imprint.

They are all relative.

I wonder how your experiences have shaped the way you are.

We are all a product of our experiences, the events that have shaped us and cause us to feel differently.

To go beyond cognitive, lets unpick what our brains actually felt.

The Rational Brain and The Emotional Brain

When we think of our brains, we tend to only think about our cognitive abilities.

In reality, it is much more than that.

Van Der Kolk writes:

"Our rational, cognitive brain is actually the youngest part of the brain and occupies only about 30% of the area inside our skull. The rational brain is concerned with the world outside us: understanding how to accomplish our goals, manage our time and sequence our actions.

"Beneath our rational brain lie two evolutionary older brains which are in charge of everything else - the identification of comfort, safety, threat, hunger, fatigue, desire, excitement, pain and pleasure."

Van der Kolk defines these two older brains, the reptilian system and the limbic system, as the *Emotional Brain*.

When we are not feeling threatened our two brains are in balance.

However, when we feel threatened, these two brains can function independently.

Have you ever tried to have a rational argument with a child who is having a meltdown?

You'll be waiting a while to win that rational argument.

In that moment, the child's emotional brain has taken over and the rational brain has taken a back seat.

Van der Kolk notes that the traditional approach by psychologists is to help people manage their behaviours through insight and understanding.

The challenge with this is that research from the field of neuroscience shows that very few psychological problems result from defects in our understanding.

In Van der Kolk's words: "when the alarm bell of the emotional brain keeps signalling that you are in danger, no amount of insight will silence it".

It is this separation of emotion and logic that creates the difficulty.

The difficulty is that trying to rationalise your way out of an emotional pattern is like using a screwdriver to hammer a nail, it's the wrong tool for the job.

Using rationality to solve a rational, cognitive problem makes perfect sense.

Using rationality to solve a problem locked in your emotional brain doesn't make sense.

Ever tried to think your way out of an emotional challenge and just got more and more frustrated going round in loops?

It's often the most challenging for highly intellectual people who are very well versed at solving cognitive problems, but in the case of emotional challenges, they can't seem to figure their way out of it.

Denial. Anger. Frustration. Distraction. Numbing (alcohol, drugs, work addictions), all point to someone trying to escape a challenge they can't think their way out of.

Sound like anyone you know?

The psychological term for what has happened leading up to this is 'dissociation'.

When we dissociate, the emotional experience is split off and fragmented so that the emotions, sounds, images, thoughts, and physical sensations take a life of their own.

As long as the trauma is not resolved, the stress emotional responses will keep being replayed when they are triggered by the memory of the original event.

Trauma Touches Us All

Dr Gabor Maté distinguishes between two types of trauma:

Big 'T' Trauma and *small 't' trauma.*

Both leave lasting marks that shape our emotional patterns.

One challenge is that when people think of trauma, they only imagine the life experiences that would lead to big 'T' Trauma, when in reality, small 't' trauma can be just as disruptive.

Let's get specific.

Capital T trauma denotes significant and severe traumatic experiences that can have a profound and long-lasting impact on an individual's life.

Capital T trauma often involves events that pose a direct threat to one's life, physical integrity, or result in extreme distress and suffering.

Some examples:

- Physical or sexual abuse
- War

- Natural disasters
- Serious accident
- Terrorist attacks
- Life-threatening illnesses

I don't think anyone would disagree that experiences like these would leave a lasting imprint capable of shaping one's behaviours.

On the other hand, Small 't' trauma refers to minor, chronic, or repetitive traumatic experiences. Remember that "*trauma is not what happens to you, it is what happens inside you*".

While the effects of small t trauma may not be as immediately obvious or extreme as those of capital T trauma, they can accumulate over time and shape the way we behave.

Examples of small 't' trauma include:

- Emotional neglect
- Bullying
- Loss of a loved one
- Divorce or parental separation
- Chronic illness or medical procedures
- Minor accidents or injuries

Small 't' trauma can affect individuals differently, and the impact may depend on various factors such as age, resilience, support, and previous experiences.

How Experiences Shape Us

The central thesis of Van der Kolk's work is that trauma affects not just the mind but also the body, and that the effects of trauma can be stored within the nervous system.

He draws on his extensive research, clinical experience, and the experiences of his patients, to present a comprehensive understanding of how trauma shapes our lives.

One of the core concepts is that of 'trauma memory'. It's how traumatic events can become stuck in the body.

An event that can be brought back by the simplest trigger.

A trigger that takes a person right back to that emotional situation where they feel the exact same emotions.

From an emotional perspective, they relive that event.

A simple example of an emotional trigger could be a person feeling a sudden surge of anxiety when they hear the sound of glass breaking. It reminds them of the fights their parents had when they were a child.

The sound serves as a reminder of the experience, and the individual's body and mind react instinctively to protect themselves, even though the present situation may not pose an immediate threat. In our daily life, we can see our responses to triggers in the self-sabotaging behaviours we find ourselves repeating, even when we 'should' know better.

Unlocking Past Emotions

The crux of the challenge in treating these triggers is that the rational brain cannot abolish emotions, sensations, and thoughts.

What makes this more complex is that understanding *why* you feel a certain way does not change *how* you feel.

The answer according to Van der Kolk is to realign our rational brain and our emotional brain: the connection that became dissociated when we experienced strong emotions.

Our emotional experiences are not just held in our cognitive brain. They are literally held within our body.

Therefore, we need to consider the whole body rather than just the brain to be able to make sense and process trapped emotions.

It's important to note that this is still a field of science in its infancy and there is much more work to be done.

Equally important is that different approaches may not work the same way for everyone, and the effectiveness can vary, depending on individual circumstances and preferences. Each person's journey is unique.

Two of the approaches I have tried, following the recommendations of these experts include:

Eye Movement Desensitization and Reprocessing (EMDR)

EMDR is an approach that involves guiding individuals to recall distressing memories while simultaneously engaging in side-to-side eye movements or other forms of bilateral stimulation.

The aim is reassociating the rational brain and the emotional brain and to allow for the processing and integration of traumatic memories. The result being to reduce the emotional impact of past experiences.

Kinesiology

Kinesiology recognises that trauma is stored in the body and can manifest as physical tension, discomfort, or disconnection.

By incorporating kinaesthetic awareness and movement into trauma therapy, individuals can develop a deeper understanding of their bodily sensations, emotions, and patterns of movement associated with trauma. This can enable the release and integration of trauma-related experiences.

Experiment for Yourself

I've shared my experiences.

I've shared some leading academics, science and writing in this space.

I invite you to run some experiments to see what this could uncover for you.

What could some experiments look like for you?

Consider talk therapy if you've not tried it before. It's a gateway to opening up a wider world of exploring our psychology and how that affects our mental health.

If you're not keen on talking, consider a notebook where you write down what strong emotions you feel. This can be a useful safety release valve.

Consider trying one of the approaches mentioned above. The Big Bold Mindset is by definition relentlessly curious and willing to run new experiments to find fresh pathways forward.

It's worth noting that the most powerful and insightful breakthroughs I've ever had with any Beyond Cognitive sessions have been when I have turned up feeling on good form like I don't have any problems and when everything has been great.

The belief that I have arrived at is that this type of work is work that never ends and that it should become a regular monthly event in the same way as we think of going to the gym several times a week.

My favourite saying in this context is:

"The cave that you don't want to go into, is the cave that you must go into".

We are only just beginning to understand how we operate as humans.

Aren't you curious to learn more about how you work and how you can optimise how you show up as a human?

It's not mainstream… yet.

Conclusion

To solve the problems of today, we need fresh thinking.

Paul Polman, the former CEO of Unilever put it well when he said," *We are still applying linear thinking to exponential problems*[33]*"*.

Linear thinking is past its sell-by-date.

We have covered so much research in this book illustrating how the ideas of yesterday are flawed and how we need a fundamental overhaul.

It starts with our mindset, the way we think.

When we think differently, we change the words and pictures in our minds.

When we change those words and pictures, we start to influence how we feel.

Together our thoughts and feelings drive different behaviours, different actions.

Different actions drive different results.

It all starts with our mindset.

The Big Bold Mindset.

---

[33] https://www.linkedin.com/posts/olibarrett_ltw2023-ltw-activity-7077276337412927488-hNVy/

What Influences Your World?

When you listen carefully to people, you can hear what influences they rely on.

You can get an insight on when they entered the working world, when their minds were wide open by the people and the theories they reference.

How many of those theories and ideas reference something fresh and new from the past one, two, five years?

Or are they outdated theories from three decades ago?

The clues are there as to what influences are likely to be acting on your team already.

The ideas of this book offer a reset button.

To hold up to the light in the face of latest thinking and research the ingrained beliefs, notions, and ideas that we all carry.

Big Bold Characteristics

Our journey to shifting our mindset has covered many areas starting with the traits and characteristics that those with a Big Bold Mindset exude.

- Adaptable - can you step outside of your comfort zone?
- Curious - ask questions
- Humble - rather than 'I am right', ask yourself, 'how do I know I'm right'
- Adventurous - daring to be different

- Analytical and open minded - willing to experiment and think like a scientist
- Reflective - taking the time to reflect
- Nurturing - thinking like a farmer
- Action Orientated - relentless action

How would you score yourself out of 1-100 on each of these areas?

Is there one area where you could pick where you would or could improve?

Why not write that down and think what you could do to increase your score in that area?

What would be your impact as a leader if you embraced these principles?

What challenges could you take on?

What difference could you make to those who you work with?

Making an Impact

Think Bigger

The first theme, the personal challenge to you was to Think Bigger.

To become aware of where you are focused; enabling you to shape an inspiring story for your team and face down impossible challenges whilst holding the myth of belief up to the light.

All actions and ideas to prime you to think the biggest and boldest you possibly can.

Leading Bigger

The second theme was around Leading Bigger - how can we lead ourselves when we want to achieve bigger and bolder goals.

Pay close attention to your influences and take control of your world.

Develop and shape your identity - this is in your control.

Know the price of ambition and pay for it in the cheapest way possible in advance.

Know that your mind runs the risk of being hijacked and take care to police it well.

Bigger Together

No big bold goal was ever achieved in isolation.

What does it take to put people first, to create a high-performance team where it's about We and not Me.

What does it take to unleash the strengths and diverse ideas from each person in your team?

How do you create that trust that is so crucial to lasting the distance to solving the hard problems?

Bigger by the Day

Prepare for the marathon, not the sprint.

Use your time dexterously from Past Present Future awareness, to focus each day on the incremental gains.

Shape your daily habits.

Build your learning rituals and have humility. Don't wait for perfect, you'll never get there.

Bigger Resilience

Setbacks will be ahead.

Forewarned is forearmed.

Do the work now to get in good shape, and by looking inward to your emotional patterns, not just outward with gritted teeth.

Find or shape the safe environment to hone your skills.

Get ready to struggle well with hard problems.

Be aware of your biases and aim to see each situation as it really is, not through the lens of inaccurate thinking.

The reward?

The reward for embracing these challenges is putting you and those around you in the best place possible to deal with the hard challenges you will inevitably face.

Doing nothing to prepare yourself for the challenges is a choice.

Make good choices and take action.

Every step in the Big Bold Mindset is doable.

The first yacht race I did was billed as ordinary people doing extraordinary things.

The only way that ordinary people, like me, get to do extraordinary things is by trying, by failing, by learning and never ever giving up.

It's your turn now.

What Now?

What's the very next experiment you are going to run?

Which chapters have resonated most with you?

Maybe pick three chapters which have hit home the most.

In the margin here or in a notebook, note down which three chapters would make the most impact in your world.

Of those three chapters, pick one.

With that one area, devise the first experiment you will run.

Now do it.

The Big Bold Mindset is about action.

Once you have mastered it and are using one area, pick the next.

Keep going and iterate forward.

Accelerating Action

Maintaining momentum is crucial.
Here's how you can make these ideas more present in your world:

Make notes of the ideas that resonate most strongly.

Put them on a wall, somewhere you will see them.

Remember, what you see is all there is.

Buy a copy of this book for your team at work. Immerse them in the thinking bigger and bolder and discuss which ideas resonate with them.

Buy a copy of this book for friends and family.

Connect with me on LinkedIn. The Big Bold Mindset is restless, inquisitive, and never done. I regularly share ideas and thoughts on what I see in the world and the impact it can have.

Consider exploring the Beyond Cognitive world for ways to create deeper lasting change.

In time, we will be releasing digital courses to go deeper into each area in this book and guide you through step by step. You can find these at www.CasparCraven.com

Book me to come and inspire and provide thought provoking ideas for your team. Contact me at caspar@casparcraven.com

Consider running the Big Bold Goals Leadership Experience to explore these ideas in depth with your team.

My Wish for You

If you have reached here, I know that we resonate with each other on some level - the messages I am fortunate enough to share are messages that will mean something to you.

My wish is that you take these ideas and put them to good use.

To make your world a better place.

To make the world a better place for those you live and work with.

To make the world a better place for all who live in it.

I wish you fun and many experiments as you explore these ideas.

To thinking, living, and acting Big and Bold.

My deepest best wishes to you,

Caspar

Resources

Books

Balcetis, Emily, Clearer, Closer, *Better: How Successful People See the World* (Ballantine Books Inc. 2020).

Bessel van der Kolk, *The Body Keeps the Score* (Penguin, 2015).

Buckingham, Marcus, *Now, Discover Your Strengths* (Simon & Schuster, 2001).

Clayton, Christensen, *The Innovator's Dilemma* (Harvard Business Review Press, 2016).

Dalio, Ray, *Principles: Life and Work* (Simon & Schuster, 2017).

Dalton-Smith, Dr. Saundra, *Sacred Rest* (FaithWords, 2019).

Damasio, Antonio, *Descartes' Error* (Vintage, 2006).

Dweck, Carol, *Mindset* (Robinson, 2017).

Gaskell, Kevin, *Inspired Leadership* (John Wiley & Sons, 2017).

Gawande, Atul, *The Checklist Manifesto* (Profile Books, 2011).
Hari, Johann, *Stolen Focus* (Bloomsbury Publishing Plc, 2022).

Kahneman, Daniel, *Thinking, Fast and Slow* (Random House, 2011).

Keller, Gary, and Jay Papasan, *The One Thing* (John Murray, 2014).

Maltz, Maxwell, *Psycho-Cybernetics* (Perigee, 2015).

Maté, Gabor, *When the Body Says No* (Vermilion, 2019).

Moss Kanter, Rosabeth, *Think Outside the Building* (Nichola Brealey Publishing, 2020).

Newport, Cal, *Deep Work* (Piatkus, 2016).

Randolph, Marc, *That Will Never Work* (Endeavour, 2021).

Sinclair, Dr David with D. LaPlante, Matthew), *Lifespan* (Harper Collins, 2019).

Waldinger, Robert, and Schulz, Marc, *The Good Life: Lessons from the World's Longest Study on Happiness* (Simon & Schuster, 2023).

Walker, Matthew, *Why We Sleep* (Penguin Books, 2018).

Articles and reports

Edmondson, Amy C, *Psychological Safety and Learning Behaviour in Work Teams*, Admin Science Quarterly, Vol 44, No, 2 (June 1999) Publ, Johnson Graduate School of Management, Cornell University, (1999).

Dorthe Kirkegaard Thomsen, Sarah E, Gaede, and Steen Kaargaard Nielsen, *Identity flexibility during adulthood: Perspectives on multidimensionality and plasticity in self-definition*, Journal of Personality and Social Psychology, Vol: 11, (2018).

Kiliç, E, & Samur, Y, *The relationship between social media use and attention performance: An investigation of the mediating role of fear of missing out*, Computers in Human Behavior, 105, 106213, (2020).

Liu, X, Hu, Y, & Chen, J, *Exploring the relationship between social media addiction and gray matter volume in a sample of Chinese college students*, Addictive Behaviors, 113, 106695, (2021).

Maher, J, P, Dunton, G, F, & Penedo, F, J, *The role of beliefs about coping effectiveness in the relationship between coping and stress*, Personality and Individual Differences, (2021).

Mckinsey Report on the Future of Jobs - https://www.mckinsey.com/featured-insights/future-of-work/jobs-lost-jobs-gained-what-the-future-of-work-will-mean-for-jobs-skills-and-wages

Mckinsey report referenced in chapter 9: The New Essentials of Employee Experience Report - https://www.mckinsey.com/capabilities/people-and-organizational-performance/our-insights/this-time-its-personal-shaping-the-new-possible-through-employee-experience

Michael Tews, Jeongyun Kim, Sean Way, and Junchao (Jason) Wang, *The impact of co-worker relationships on work outcomes: A meta-analytic review and future research agenda by Publication,* Journal of Business and Psychology, (2021).

Nien-hê Hsieh, Joe J, Broschak, and Zachary Mohr, *Organizational Ethical Culture and Financial Performance: A Meta-Analysis,* Journal of Business Ethics, (2021).

Publication in the Journal of Personality and Social Psychology (2010) referenced in chapter 7 on science of support

University of Georgia research published in the Journal of Marriage and Family (2017) referenced in Chapter 7 on Science of Support

Yeager, D, S, Dweck, C, S, & Trzesniewski, K, H, *An implicit theory of personality predicts motivation and goal progress across adulthood,* Journal of Personality and Social Psychology, (2020).

Yougov survey of senior managers: https://www.thetimes.co.uk/article/high-flyers-pay-a-price-in-misery-at-home-ggctmcb68

Zak, P.J, *The Neuroscience of Trust,* https://hbr,org/2017/01/the-neuroscience-of-trust

Zenger, J, H, & Folkman, J, *The impact of peer advisory groups on CEO's social support, learning and personal growth,* Journal of Business and Psychology, (2020).

https://hbr.org/2012/09/ten-reasons-people-resist-chang

https://business.wisc.edu/news/leadership-gems-from-tiaa-ceo-thasunda-brown-duckett

https://www.insiderintelligence.com/insights/us-time-spent-with-media

https://www.hibamagazine.com/screen-dependency-disorder

https://hbr.org/2018/01/what-self-awareness-really-is-and-how-to-cultivate-it

https://universitycollegeblog.du.edu/2021/07/leadership-skills-to-reduce-workplace-drama-and-drive-results

https://hbr.org/2019/11/the-best-performing-ceos-in-the-world-2019

https://www.thestreet.com/investing/stocks/nvidia-jensen-huang-businessperson-of-the-year-14393724

https://www.ucl.ac.uk/news/2009/aug/how-long-does-it-take-form-habit

https://www.ncbi.nlm.nih.gov/pmc/articles/PMC6529595/-Nature Communications 2020

https://www.frontiersin.org/articles/10.3389/fnins.2021.630829/full

https://hbr.org/2018/12/the-pros-and-cons-of-perfectionism-according-to-research

https://www.lse.ac.uk/research/research-for-the-world/health/over-stressed-and-under-pressure-the-problem-with-being-perfect

https://www.thecorporategovernanceinstitute.com/insights/news-analysis/ceos-are-burned-out-and-leaving

https://hbr.org/2022/03/hbs-professor-linda-hill-says-leaders-must-engage-with-emotions-as-never-before

https://www.youtube.com/watch?v=WXuK6gekU1Y

https://hbr.org/2023/05/why-conflicting-ideas-can-make-your-strategy-stronger?ab=HP-hero-latest-text-1

https://www.gsb.stanford.edu/insights/pepsi-ceo-break-past-dont-play-too-nice

https://www.worldfinance.com/special-reports.how-indra-nooyi-changed-the-face-of-pepsico

https://www.linkedin.com/posts/olibarrett_ltw2023-ltw-activity-7077276337412927488-hNVy

Interviews

Lore, Marc, *Has Marc Lore Discovered the Secret to Entrepreneurship*? https://www.inc.com/magazine/202212/tom-foster/has-marc-lore-discovered-secret-entrepreneurship.html

Perkins, Melanie, 8 Lessons From Melanie Perkins, https://www.forbes.com/sites/dileeprao/2023/02/09/unicorn-entrepreneurship-8-lessons-from-melanie-perkins-of-canva/?sh=4318b00879dd

Saujani, Reshma, Interview with CNBC on work-life integration, https://www.cnbc.com/2021/02/25/tech-ceo-reshma-saujani-calls-for-2400-monthly-stimulus-to-moms.html

Sarah Blakely, Interview with Forbes magazine, https://www.forbes.com/sites/elanagross/2021/11/29/spanx-founder-sara-blakely-shares-her-best-advice-for-entrepreneurs-at-the-forbes-next-1000-summit/?sh=4aaba9eb3141

Jeff Weiner, Interview with Forbes magazine, https://www.forbes.com/sites/jeannemeister/2012/09/10/10-leadership-lessons-from-jeff-weiner-ceo-of-linkedin/?sh=586d76c639a4

Websites

Rich Roll https://www.richroll,com
Tom Bilyeu https://impacttheory.com/
Dr. Ranjan Chatterjee https://drchatterjee.com
Andrew Huberman https://hubermanlab.com

Printed in Great Britain
by Amazon

29826450R00182